# Jesus Christ in the Preaching of Calvin and Schleiermacher

# COLUMBIA SERIES IN REFORMED THEOLOGY

The Columbia Series in Reformed Theology represents a joint commitment of Columbia Theological Seminary and Westminster John Knox Press to provide theological resources for the church today.

The Reformed tradition has always sought to discern what the living God revealed in scripture is saying and doing in every new time and situation. Volumes in this series examine significant individuals, events, and issues in the development of this tradition and explore their implications for contemporary Christian faith and life.

This series is addressed to scholars, pastors, and laypersons. The Editorial Board hopes that these volumes will contribute to the continuing reformation of the church.

## EDITORIAL BOARD

Shirley Guthrie, Columbia Theological Seminary

George Stroup, Columbia Theological Seminary

Donald K. McKim, Memphis Theological Seminary

B. A. Gerrish, University of Chicago

Amy Plantinga Pauw,
Louisville Presbyterian Theological Seminary

Columbia Theological Seminary wishes to express its appreciation to the following churches for supporting this joint publishing venture:

First Presbyterian Church, Tupelo, Mississippi

First Presbyterian Church, Nashville, Tennessee

Trinity Presbyterian Church, Atlanta, Georgia

Spring Hill Presbyterian Church, Mobile, Alabama

St. Stephen Presbyterian Church, Fort Worth, Texas

COLUMBIA SERIES IN REFORMED THEOLOGY

# Jesus Christ in the Preaching of Calvin and Schleiermacher

## DAWN DeVRIES

 Westminster John Knox Press
Louisville, Kentucky

Scripture quotations, except where noted, are from the New Revised Standard Version of the Bible, copyright © 1989 by the Division of Christian Education of the National Council of the Churches of Christ in the U.S.A., and used by permission.

*Book and cover design by Drew Stevens*

*First edition*

Published by Westminster John Knox Press
Louisville, Kentucky

This book is printed on acid-free paper that meets the American National Standards Institute Z39.48 standard. ∞

PRINTED IN THE UNITED STATES OF AMERICA

96 97 98 99 00 01 02 03 04 05 — 10 9 8 7 6 5 4 3 2 1

**Library of Congress Cataloging-in-Publication Data**

DeVries, Dawn, date–
    Jesus Christ in the preaching of Calvin and Schleiermacher / Dawn DeVries. — 1st ed.
        p.      cm. — (Columbia series in Reformed theology)
    Includes bibliographical references and index.
    ISBN 0-664-22067-3 (alk. paper)
    1. Jesus Christ — History of doctrines—16th century.   2. Jesus Christ—History of doctrines—18th century.   3. Jesus Christ—History of doctrines—19th century.   4. Preaching—History—16th century.   5. Preaching—History—18th century.   6. Preaching—History—19th century.   7. Bible. N.T. Gospels—Homiletical use. 8. Calvin, Jean, 1509–1564.   9. Schleiermacher, Friedrich, 1768–1834.   I. Title.   II. Series.
    BT198.D48    1996
    232'.092'2—dc20                                              96–540

*For Brian*
*a Calvinist of a higher order*

# CONTENTS

# ABBREVIATIONS

CO          *Ioannis Calvini opera quae supersunt omnia*

ET          English translation

Gl.         *Der christliche Glaube nach den Grundsätzen der evangelischen Kirche im Zusammenhange dargestellt* (1830–31)

Inst.       *Institutes of the Christian Religion* (1559)

KD          *Kurze Darstellung des theologischen Studiums zum Behuf einleitender Vorlesungen*

KGA         *F.D.E. Schleiermacher: Kritische Gesamtausgabe*

OS          *Ioannis Calvini opera selecta*

PT          *Die praktische Theologie nach den Grundsätzen der evangelischen Kirche im Zusammenhange dargestellt*

Reden       *Friedrich Schleiermachers Reden über die Religion*

Sendschreiben   *Schleiermachers Sendschreiben über seine Glaubenslehre an Lücke*

SW          *Friedrich Schleiermachers sämmtliche Werke*

# PREFACE

My interest in the present study is not to explore every christological question that could be considered in relation to Calvin's and Schleiermacher's sermons, but rather to answer a more limited question: namely, of what importance is the Jesus of history, and what we can know about him, to the preaching of Calvin and Schleiermacher? The title of the dissertation on which this book is based, *Christus Praesens: Word and History in the Preaching of John Calvin and Friedrich Schleiermacher*, was more precise but was deemed a little esoteric. It is the Christ present in the proclaimed Word (the *Christus praesens*) that is the center of both Calvin's and Schleiermacher's preaching. This, at least, is what the present study sets out to show.

I am grateful to the readers who evaluated this manuscript for Westminster John Knox Press: David Bartlett, Jack Forstman, and Donald McKim. They each brought to my attention aspects of my argument that needed further development or fine-tuning, and they also made helpful concrete suggestions for improvements.

My work has also profited from the careful reading of some friends. John Burkhart pointed out weaknesses in the argument and gaps in the supporting evidence that I hope I have addressed. Bruce McCormack, who is still waiting for my written response to his generous letter of critique, urged me not to be too hasty in attributing motives to Barth's reading of Schleiermacher when I certainly did not have the evidence for reconstructing them. I have tried, as he cautioned me, not to demonize Barth in the process of recovering the evangelical Schleiermacher for the Reformed tradition. Whether I have succeeded is for the reader to decide. My friend and former pastor Harry Arnold read my manuscript carefully and pointed out some slips I was happy to correct. But more than that, he first taught me the power of the preached Word and nurtured my incipient love of theology. Although I am sure he would not agree with everything I say in this book, I hope I have not disappointed him.

The argument of this book was a long time in the making, and it benefited from conversations with many of my student colleagues at the

University of Chicago. In particular, I am grateful to Barbara Pitkin, Linda Lee Nelson, Julia Lamm, Mary Stimming, Eric Crump, Paul Capetz, and Bob Sherman.

My thanks also extend to Professor James Kay, whose argument concerning Bultmann's Christology (*Christus Praesens: A Reconsideration of Rudolf Bultmann's Christology* [Grand Rapids: Eerdmans, 1994]) might be usefully compared to what I argue about Calvin and Schleiermacher in the present study. He was kind enough to share a copy of his book with me, and we had some good conversation about the sacramental Word during my visit to Princeton in the spring of 1994.

My last debt is also my greatest one—to my husband of five years, and my teacher and friend of fourteen years. When I first arrived at the University of Chicago as an undergraduate in 1981, I was convinced that I had lost my faith, but at the same time I knew that a life with no faith was intolerable. My relentless search for something to replace the faith of my childhood led me from music to medieval studies and, through a series of providential serendipities, finally to Brian Gerrish's classroom. It was there that I first discovered a way back to my tradition. He taught me the difference between Calvin and Calvinists and introduced me to a great German Reformed theologian whose name I had never heard before. For me he has been an inspiring teacher, a valuable mentor, an honest critic, a fascinating conversation partner, a faithful friend, and now, more recently, also a loving husband and father to our daughter. In gratitude for all he has given me, and with profound respect and love, I dedicate this book to him.

# 1

# THE HISTORIAN
# AND THE PREACHER

It is a very high commendation of the Holy Scriptures, that we must not seek anywhere else the wisdom that is sufficient for salvation. . . . But at the same time the apostle states what we ought to seek in Scripture; for the false prophets also make use of it as a pretext; and so, in order that it may be useful to us for salvation, we have to know how to use it rightly.

Calvin, *Commentary on 2 Timothy*, 3:15

When rightly understood, the infinite significance of the Holy Scripture is not in contradiction to its hermeneutical limitations.
Schleiermacher, *Aphorisms on Hermeneutics*

While the effects of historical criticism on *theology* in the modern period have been well documented, their implications for post-Enlightenment *preaching* have been largely ignored. The difficult position of the minister in a postcritical world was perceived acutely by one of historical criticism's greatest champions, David Friedrich Strauss (1808–74). Could a minister, he asked, any longer preach in good conscience on Gospel narratives that very likely did not relate historical facts? Strauss considered four alternatives for preachers faced with this predicament, and only the last one was a real option. First, preachers could try to raise their hearers to their own consciousness, so that their congregations would not be disturbed by the possibility that the Gospels were fiction. But this would be impracticable, since not everyone in the church is theologically sophisticated. Second, they could try to lower themselves to the church's consciousness and preach as if all the stories were true. But then they would be hypocrites. Third, they could leave the ministry, which is clearly a desperate course and a last resort. The only feasible course for preachers to take, then, is a fourth option—to reconcile their own consciousness and the consciousness of the church. This can be accomplished, Strauss argues, by interpreting the biblical narratives in moral or doctrinal categories. And oddly enough, he contends, it is precisely in undertaking this kind of interpretation that orthodox and speculative preaching converge. No matter if orthodox preachers, unlike speculative preachers, still *assume* that the history related in the narratives is true. The very fact that they too proceed from history to doctrine implies at least this much: "The history is not enough, it is not the whole truth, it must be transmuted from a past fact into a present one, from an event foreign and external to you, it must become your own inner fact of experience."[1]

Strauss's contention that precritical preaching and postcritical preaching do virtually the same thing provides an interesting point of entry into the question of the relationship between classical and liberal Protestantism. How much difference did historical criticism actually make to the way Christ was preached in the church? Were liberal preachers only beating a hasty retreat when they moved from the "external" miracles of the Gospel narratives to the "internal" miracle of faith? Or were they also following a path already opened up by their predecessors? These are the questions that will be explored in this book through a comparison of the preaching of John Calvin and the preaching of Friedrich Schleiermacher on the Gospel narratives.

I will argue that Schleiermacher's understanding of preaching as, in effect, an incarnational event that re-presents the person and work of the Jesus of history may be seen as a genuine development of Calvin's notion of the sacramental Word, a development that made possible a relative indifference to doubts about the historical facts of the life of Jesus.[2] In fact, the assaults of historical criticism in the eighteenth and nineteenth centuries on the Gospel narratives did not force Schleiermacher to retreat from the claims of precritical theology about the redemptive power of Jesus Christ, but rather encouraged him to apply Reformation principles more radically and consistently.

My argument will be operating on two levels. Construed narrowly, the thesis attempts to contribute something to the interpretation of the respective theologies of Calvin and Schleiermacher. More broadly, it makes a historical assertion about doctrinal development in the Protestant tradition. In this introduction, I want to consider the contexts within the scholarly literature for each of these aspects of my argument.

## WORD AS SACRAMENT IN THE THEOLOGY
## OF JOHN CALVIN

Although there is a significant body of literature on Calvin's doctrine of the Word of God, there is a surprising absence of any detailed treatment of how the *preached* Word functions within this doctrine—surprising because the central importance of the preached Word in Calvin's theology has been generally recognized.[3] There are several possible explanations for this gap in the literature. First, much of the literature on Calvin's doctrine of the Word of God seems to be calculated to support one or another contemporary form of Reformed theology, particularly on the issues of biblical inspiration and authority.[4] The problem with this approach is that contemporary questions may not be the most instructive ones to address to Calvin. The inspiration and authority of scripture were simply not problematic for Calvin as they are for us. While Calvin does indeed speak of the Word as the sole sufficient source and norm of faith and doctrine, he also frequently speaks of the Word as the *instrument* of our communion with Christ—the Word as sacrament.[5] Ernst Bizer has argued that in Luther's theology the sacraments are understood verbally and, correspondingly, the Word itself takes on a sacramental character.[6] The same argument might be made of Calvin's theology. And in explicating what Calvin means when he speaks of the Word as the means by which Jesus Christ is dispensed to us, we may be coming closer to his own concerns than we do when we concentrate on whether he held a mechanical or an organic theory of inspiration.

A second possible explanation for the absence of literature on the role of the preached Word in Calvin's doctrine of the Word of God is the complexity of the issues involved. If, according to Calvin, the preached Word is sacramental—if it "dispenses Jesus Christ"—then one needs to consider simultaneously Calvin's doctrines of scripture and the sacraments, his theory of preaching, his Christology, and his hermeneutics in order to explain what he meant by the preached Word. By and large, the Calvin literature has treated these topics discretely.[7] Bringing the various loci together again may not be a simple task, but the systematic character of Calvin's thought requires it.

A final possible explanation for the gap in the literature has to do with Calvin's failure to furnish an extended discussion of his theory of the sacramental Word. Like his concept of inspiration and his biblical hermeneutic, Calvin's understanding of the Word as sacrament is assumed throughout his work but is discussed explicitly only in brief and disconnected passages scattered randomly in his writings.[8] In order to develop a persuasive explanation of his theory, it is not enough simply to string together everything he says about the sacramental Word.[9] In addition, one must observe Calvin's own preaching and infer what the operative principles behind it are.

One important aim of my argument, then, is to fill this gap in the literature. In the second chapter, I analyze Calvin's notion of the sacramental Word, giving particular attention to the ways in which he speaks of the real presence of Christ in the church's proclamation. Chapter 3 explores Calvin's own method of "administering" the sacramental Word in his sermons on the Synoptic Gospels. The goal in this chapter is not to describe the content of these sermons in detail but to illustrate Calvin's homiletic strategy for dealing with the Gospel narratives and to determine to what extent a consistent strategy controlled his use of the texts. This chapter provides the groundwork for a comparison with Schleiermacher's sermons on the same texts.

## FRIEDRICH SCHLEIERMACHER:
## A THEOLOGIAN OF THE WORD?

The situation I am addressing in the scholarly literature on Schleier-macher is somewhat different from the problems with the Calvin literature I described above. There is not simply a gap—a relative neglect of one particular issue—in the treatment of his doctrine of the Word; rather, the Word-centered character of Schleiermacher's theology has been almost universally ignored or misinterpreted. The problem became particularly acute in the opening decades of this century, when Karl Barth and Emil Brunner launched the neo-orthodox offensive against Schleiermacher's theology. One of the chief points of their critique was that Schleiermacher allegedly failed to preserve the Reformation emphasis on the Word as the source and norm of Christian faith.[10] Unfortunately, it could be argued that Schleiermacher's own methodological prolegomena are responsible, at least in part, for this misinterpretation. He argued for a careful distinction between dogmatics and exegesis, and hence biblical language is not the subject matter of his *Glaubenslehre*.[11] Further, Schleiermacher maintains that dogmatics describes not articles of belief but the consciousness of believers.[12] It is not impossible to see how Barth and Brunner might have regarded Schleiermacher's dogmatics as bereft of the Word. What they failed to recognize, however, is that Schleiermacher held on firmly to the very understanding of the Word that the Reformers themselves treasured: the efficacious Word as sacrament, the Word that "presents Christ." It is the task of chapter 4 to support this claim by analyzing Schleiermacher's theory of preaching, showing how the preached Word functions in his theology, and demonstrating parallels with Calvin's concept of the sacramental Word.

Although a major aim of my thesis as it deals with Schleiermacher is to correct the neo-orthodox misunderstanding of his theology of the Word, I will also attempt to fill a gap in the literature by discussing Schleiermacher's sermons on the Synoptic Gospels. His sermons represent one third of his published writings, yet the secondary literature, until recently, has paid them only scant attention.[13] The goal in chapter 5 is much the same as that in chapter 3 on Calvin's sermons: to uncover the homiletic strategy Schleiermacher uses in dealing with the Gospel narratives. I will conclude by drawing the comparison with Calvin, and by suggesting how Schleiermacher's method may be seen as formally parallel to Calvin's method.

## LIBERAL THEOLOGY AND THE LEGACY
## OF THE REFORMATION

One of the most sharply debated issues in twentieth-century theology has been how we are to interpret the revolution that occurred in the theology of the nineteenth century. Was Protestant liberalism a wholesale abandonment of the theology of the Reformers? Did liberal doctrinal developments actually change in essence the character of Christian faith? Did liberal theologians pretend to speak about God when they were in fact speaking about humanity in exalted tones?[14] These questions seem to be no closer to receiving conclusive answers now than when they were initially voiced during the first quarter of this century.[15] And, not surprisingly, the interpretation of Schleiermacher is at the center of much of the debate. My intention here is, in part, to contribute to this assessment of Protestant liberalism's relationship to the Reformation. Specifically, I seek to show that Schleiermacher's doctrine of the Word of God is not only at the center of his own dogmatic system, but also can be seen as a faithful development from Calvin's doctrine of the Word.[16] In order to establish this claim, however, I will have to answer those critics who read Schleiermacher's relationship to Calvin differently than I do.

The neo-orthodox interpreters of Schleiermacher, and their present-day disciples, have been the most consistent in maintaining that his theology represents a significant deviation from, or distortion of, the theology of classical Protestantism. Their critique is many-sided and thoroughgoing, and it would be both impossible and undesirable to address it fully within the limits of this study. Yet though these critics touch on numerous points of doctrine, their objections may perhaps admit of a simple schematization. Two basic types of accusations are leveled against Schleiermacher: that he eliminated from his theological system doctrines essential to the theology of the Reformers, and that he allowed something outside the province of Christian belief (e.g., science, philosophy, or historical criticism) to control and limit his expression even of the doctrines he included. The first type of criticism accuses liberal theology of abandoning the regulative themes of the Reformers, while the second sees it as a distortion of them. Throughout this study, I attempt to respond to two critics of Schleiermacher's doctrine of the Word, each of whom may be taken to represent one of these two types of criticism: Karl Barth and Hans Frei.

Barth's fundamental criticism of Schleiermacher's doctrine of the Word is simple to state: There *is* none. From his 1923–24 lectures on

Schleiermacher's theology at Göttingen University to his "Concluding Unscientific Postscript on Schleiermacher" of 1968, Barth consistently maintained that Schleiermacher falsely substituted the word of man for the Word of God, anthropology for Christology.[17] "Nothing remained," Barth tells us, "of the belief that the Word or statement is as such the bearer, bringer, and proclaimer of truth, that there might be such a thing as the Word of God. Schleiermacher knows the concept of the *kerygma*, but naturally a kerygma that only *depicts* and does not *bring*, that only *states* or *expresses* and does not *declare*."[18] The absence of objective revelation, of the Word "coming from God's side," Barth argued, forced Schleiermacher to depart significantly from the theology of the Reformers. And though Schleiermacher claimed he drew his idea of an "eternal covenant" between science and theology from the Reformers' thought, Barth insists that "their goal was a different one from that assigned to them by Schleiermacher."[19] For the Reformers, Barth informs us, the Word was still the *subject*, and not the *predicate*, of theology.

It is tempting to dismiss Barth's charges without further consideration when one sees how often he misquotes or takes out of context what Schleiermacher actually said.[20] To do so, however, would be to treat Barth no better than Barth himself treated Schleiermacher. In my chapters on Schleiermacher, then, I try to answer Barth's objections, always presupposing that there may be some real and serious problems in Schleiermacher's position. My response to Barth is twofold: Schleiermacher *did* give up part of Calvin's doctrine of the Word—the same part that Barth himself abandoned, that is, Calvin's biblicism; at the same time, Schleiermacher maintained and developed Calvin's notion of the sacramental Word, and Barth himself recognizes that this concept is an essential part of the legacy of the Reformation.[21]

The spokesman for the second line of criticism—that alien influences led to a distortion in Schleiermacher's understanding of the Word—is Hans Frei. Frei's work is more subtle and carefully documented than is Barth's, and hence it will require greater effort to challenge it. Frei's thesis can be stated as follows: Precritical interpretative procedures for isolating the "realistic" element in biblical narratives broke down irretrievably with the development of historical criticism in the eighteenth and nineteenth centuries, and hence the realistic narrative reading of the biblical stories went into eclipse.[22] Frei identifies three such interpretative procedures (or, one might say, "presuppositions") in the "precritical" hermeneutics. First, it always assumed that the biblical story "referred to and described actual historical occurrences." Second, since it assumed that the various biblical stories described a single real world of one temporal sequence, the precritical hermeneutics sought for a way to unite these various narratives into one cumulative story. This it accomplished by means of figuration or typology. Third, since it assumed that "the world truly rendered by combining the biblical narratives into one was indeed the one and only real world, [it claimed that] it must in principle embrace the experience of any present age and reader."[23] These presuppositions were challenged and finally abandoned as a result of the development of historical criticism, and, accordingly, Frei perceives a wide gap between the ways in which the Reformers and the Protestant liberals read biblical narratives.

Frei's thesis, of course, is intended to apply to a much larger cast of characters than simply Calvin and Schleiermacher, and I could not pretend to disprove it by restricting my analysis to these two thinkers. Nonetheless, I wish to question a fundamental part of his thesis by asking: Do Calvin and Schleiermacher really fit into this scheme? Frei takes Calvin as the example par excellence of "precritical" interpretation.[24] More than Luther, Calvin had a "sense of the subject matter of scripture being constituted by or identical with its narrative."[25] The subject matter of the text for Calvin, Frei argues, cannot be separated from the text itself; moreover, the literal explicative sense was perceived by Calvin to be identical with its actual historical reference. Thus, Frei claims, Calvin regarded the task of the interpreter to be simply that of comprehending the meaning that is seen in, or emerges from, the cumulative sequence of the narrative.[26]

The task of interpretation according to Schleiermacher, Frei maintains, was something quite different. Schleiermacher thought that the subject matter was fully separable from the biblical texts. Hence, for him the narratives referred to something else—to historical events, to ideas, or to consciousness—and so meant something different from what they said.[27] For this reason, Frei argues, Schleiermacher had no means for making sense of the narrative structure of the life of Jesus as presented in the Gospels— a weakness in his hermeneutics that is manifestly evident in his anticlimactic interpretation of the "death" of Jesus as only in appearance (a *Scheintod*).[28]

My response to Frei's thesis is three-sided. First, I try to show that Calvin does not fit easily into the mold of "precritical" interpreter, in Frei's sense of that term. Calvin often goes beyond the mere words and narrative structure of the text to ask questions that would be ruled out by a strictly narrative reading.[29] Moreover, Calvin's homiletic strategy in preaching on biblical narratives seems to assume precisely the opposite situation from that presupposed by "precritical" interpreters: he starts from the fact that biblical narratives cannot in themselves embrace our experience but must be "accommodated" or translated for our own situation.[30] Second, I seek to show that Frei has fundamentally misinterpreted Schleiermacher by failing to take account of his division of the theological disciplines, which he spells out clearly in his *Brief Outline on the Study of Theology*. Third, I argue that what Frei calls the "realistic" reading of biblical narratives maintained a place of importance in Christian *preaching* in the liberal Protestant tradition. The "eclipse" Frei sees in eighteenth- and nineteenth-century interpretations of the Bible is at best a partial one—an eclipse of narrative interpretations of the texts in technical biblical scholarship. For Calvin, there was little or no difference between the task of the preacher and the task of the commentator, while for Schleiermacher these tasks had fundamentally different goals and methods.[31] For all these reasons, I conclude that Frei's thesis, at least as it relates to Calvin and Schleiermacher, cannot be accepted without significant qualifications.

I must, however, quickly add a note of caution about this aspect of my argument. I am not saying that Schleiermacher is the *only* legitimate heir to the Reformed tradition, nor even that he is the most adequate one. To make such an argument would require far more engagement with other inheritors of the Reformed tradition than is necessary to achieve my more modest goal. I am neither denying nor affirming that Karl Barth and Hans Frei represent, in their own ways, faithful trajectories from the theology of the Reformation. I am simply disagreeing with their reading of Schleiermacher and his relationship to the theology of Calvin, specifically their disinheritance of him as a Reformed theologian.

## CHRISTOLOGY AND THE HISTORICAL JESUS: WHAT IS THE SUBJECT OF CHRISTOLOGY?

There is no question that the rise of historical criticism led to a crisis for Christology. D. F. Strauss posed to Schleiermacher what he, Strauss, had come to see as a decisive choice: Will Christology speak of the Christ of faith or the Jesus of history? There can be no both/and, Strauss contends, for "the ideal of the dogmatic Christ on the one hand and the historical Jesus of Nazareth on the other are irrevocably separated."[32] Whether or not Strauss was right to distinguish so sharply between the alternatives, his assessment of the situation seems to be still pertinent to contemporary theology, for there is still a division between those who take the historical Jesus to be the subject of Christology and those who do not. Among the latter, however, there is no single answer to the question, What then *is* the subject of Christology? In presenting Schleiermacher's answer to this question, I intend to show that his Christology may still be pertinent to contemporary constructive theology.

Chapter 6 discusses the relationship between Schleiermacher's understanding of the sacramental Word and his Christology. I argue that the subject of Christology, for Schleiermacher, is neither the historical Jesus nor the "ideal Christ" of the church's dogma. Rather, Christology has its point of departure in the church's proclamation—in the Christ who is *present* in the Word. This move is theologically significant for at least three reasons. First, in continuity with his Reformed heritage, Schleiermacher places the Word of God at the center of his system. While the "christomorphic" character of Schleiermacher's theology has been generally recognized, few interpreters have gone the next step to acknowledge that Schleiermacher's Christology has its source in the proclamation of Christ.[33] But this acknowledgment is crucial, for it is precisely in his emphasis on the preached Word that Schleiermacher maintains a strong connection with classical Protestantism.

Second, Schleiermacher's revision of Christology effectively averts the question of the historical Jesus—at least as it applies to the doctrine of the work of Christ—while at the same time maintaining the positivity of revelation. The work of Christ does not refer to an act of appeasing God's wrath that took place in the life of the Jesus of history, but rather to an "influence" of the *Christus praesens* on the believer in the present. Schleiermacher simply moves his anchor point in history from the distant past of the church's origins to the present reality of the church's proclamation. Finally, because of this move to the *Christus praesens,* Schleiermacher is more able than Calvin to formulate coherently the relationship between Christology and soteriology. Calvin's entire soteriology is based on the notion of a union with Christ that is effected by the work of the Holy Spirit through the Word and faith. Although he is clear in insisting that this union is necessary for salvation, Calvin is, however, unclear about how it relates to the objective, and presumably self-sufficient, "work" of Christ that he set out in Book 2 of his *Institutes.*[34] Schleiermacher, on the contrary, defines the work of the Redeemer from beginning to end in terms of a necessary union of Christ and the believer. And while, like Calvin, he argues that this union with Christ requires a conjunction of Word, faith, and Spirit, Schleiermacher is better able than Calvin to explain this conjunction as a hermeneutic event that entails a human act of interpretation. The preacher's words "embody" the Word; that is, preaching becomes the continuing locus for the ongoing redemptive work of Christ.

Schleiermacher's revisionary Christology is not, to be sure, without problems of its own. His attempt to reformulate the Chalcedonian definition of the person of Christ by substituting the terms "ideal" and "actual" for "divine" and "human" finally founders on the same rocks of historicism that Schleiermacher rightly identified as bringing about the demise of the old orthodoxy.[35] And if we take with utmost seriousness his pioneering *Lectures on the Life of Jesus,* we must conclude that Schleiermacher *did* believe that the efficacy of the church's proclamation of Christ—and hence of the *Christus praesens*—depends on a minimum of assured information about the historical person who gave rise to the church's preaching.[36] One cannot ignore these difficulties in Schleiermacher's position. Yet, I will argue in conclusion, a Christology of the *Christus praesens* may perhaps still be a useful alternative for contemporary theology.

## NOTES

1. David Friedrich Strauss, *Das Leben Jesu, kritisch bearbeitet*, 2 vols. (Tübingen: Verlag C. F. Osiander, 1835–36), 2:740–43. (ET, *The Life of Jesus Critically Examined*, trans. George Eliot, 4th ed., ed. Peter C. Hodgson [reprint, Philadelphia: Fortress Press, 1972], 782–84.)

2. The descriptive term "incarnational event" is my own, and perhaps at least an initial definition of it is necessary here. Schleiermacher argues that the preached Word not only conveys Christ to the believing hearer but also "embodies" the *Christus praesens*. Thus, in a very real sense preaching is an enfleshment of the Word.

3. See, for example, Ronald S. Wallace, *Calvin's Doctrine of the Word and Sacrament* (Edinburgh: Oliver & Boyd, 1953), 82–89. Erwin Mülhaupt, in his *Die Predigt Calvins, ihre Geschichte, ihre Form und ihre religiösen Grundgedanken*, Arbeiten zur Kirchengeschichte, vol. 18 (Berlin and Leipzig: Walter de Gruyter, 1931), restricts his discussion, for the most part, to Calvin's own practice in preaching, although he does analyze briefly Calvin's theory of preaching (pp. 24–38). Similarly, T.H.L. Parker's *The Oracles of God: An Introduction to the Preaching of John Calvin* (London and Redhill: Lutterworth, 1947) is primarily concerned with the historical background and not with the function of preaching in Calvin's doctrine of the Word, although he does make some brief comments on this subject (pp. 49–56). The secondary literature will be discussed more fully in chapter 2.

4. H. Jackson Forstman, in his *Word and Spirit: Calvin's Doctrine of Biblical Authority* (Stanford, Calif.: Stanford University Press, 1962), points to this problem in his introduction, where he singles out three categories for interpreting Calvin's understanding of biblical authority (pp. 4–5), which may in fact correspond roughly to three contemporary positions on the question. Forstman does not draw this conclusion himself, but it seems justified.

5. See, for example, his *Petit traicté de la Saincte Cene de nostre Seigneur Iesus Christ* (1541) in *Ioannis Calvini opera quae supersunt omnia*, ed. Wilhelm Baum, Edward Cunitz, Edward Reuss, 59 vols., in *Corpus Reformatorum*, vols. 29–87 (Brunswick: C. A. Schwetschke and Son, 1863–1900), 5:435. Hereafter cited as *CO*. See also John Calvin, *Institutio Christianae religionis*, ed. Peter Barth, Wilhelm Niesel, and Dora Scheuner, in *Ioannis Calvini opera selecta*, vols. 3–5 (Munich: Chr. Kaiser Verlag, 1926–52), 1.11.3, 2.10.7, 4.14.17, 4.14.26 (cited by book, chapter, and section). Hereafter cited as *Inst.* Volume and page numbers, where added in parentheses following ET, refer to the standard English translation, *Calvin: Institutes of the Christian Religion*, trans. Ford Lewis Battles, ed. John T. McNeill, Library of Christian Classics, vols. 20–21 (Philadelphia: Westminster Press, 1960); I do not, however, always give Battles's translation of citations within the text.

6. *Fides ex auditu: Eine Untersuchung über die Entdeckung der Gerechtigkeit Gottes durch Martin Luther* (Neukirchen: Verlag der Buchhandlung des Erziehungsvereins, 1958), 160.

7. There are, of course, important exceptions to this generalization. See, for example, Wallace, *Calvin's Doctrine of the Word and Sacrament*, v; B. A. Gerrish, "Gospel and Eucharist: John Calvin on the Lord's Supper," in *The Old Protestantism and the New* (Chicago: University of Chicago Press, 1982), 106–17.

8. See Forstman, 5, 49; Alexandre Ganoczy and Stefan Scheld, *Die Hermeneutik Calvins: Geistesgeschichtliche Voraussetzungen und Grundzüge*, Veröffentlichungen des Instituts für Europäische Geschichte Mainz, vol. 114 (Wiesbaden: Franz Steiner Verlag, 1983), 106–7.

9. This is a common tendency in the interpretation of other themes in Calvin's theology. See, for example, Wallace, *Calvin's Doctrine of the Word and Sacrament*; Leroy Nixon, *John Calvin, Expository Preacher* (Grand Rapids: Wm. B. Eerdmans Publishing Co., 1950).

10. See Heinrich Emil Brunner, *Die Mystik und das Wort: Der Gegensatz zwischen moderner Religionsauffassung und christlichem Glauben dargestellt an der Theologie Schleiermachers* (Tübingen: J.C.B. Mohr, 1924). For a discussion of Brunner's critique of Schleiermacher, see B. A. Gerrish, *Tradition and the Modern World: Reformed Theology in the Nineteenth Century* (Chicago: University of Chicago Press, 1978), 13–48, esp. 22–29. Barth never attempted the kind of sustained systematic critique of Schleiermacher that Brunner did, but arguing with various doctrines in Schleiermacher's system was to become a lifelong obsession for him. See note 17 below. For one of his earliest public statements of this kind, see his address, "Das Wort Gottes als Aufgabe der Theologie," in Karl Barth, *Das Wort Gottes und die Theologie* (Munich: Chr. Kaiser Verlag, 1924), 156–78, esp. 164–65.

11. See Friedrich Schleiermacher, *Kurze Darstellung des theologischen Studiums zum Behuf einleitender Vorlesungen*, 3d, critical ed., ed. Heinrich Scholz (reprint ed., Darmstadt: Wissenschaftliche Buchgesellschaft, 1961), § 85, where he divides historical theology into three separate fields: exegesis, church history, and dogmatics. Hereafter cited as *KD*. Page numbers for ET refer to the standard English translation, *Brief Outline on the Study of Theology*, trans. Terrence N. Tice (Richmond: John Knox Press, 1966). See also Friedrich Schleiermacher, *Der christliche Glaube nach den Grundsätzen der evangelischen Kirche im Zusammenhange dargestellt*, 7th ed., based on the 2d German ed., ed. Martin Redeker, 2 vols. (Berlin: Walter de Gruyter, 1960), § 27. Hereafter cited as *Gl*. Page numbers following ET refer to the standard English translation, *The Christian Faith*, trans. from the 2d German ed., ed. H. R. Mackintosh and J. S. Stewart (Philadelphia: Fortress Press, 1976). A further reason for the exclusion of biblical language from the dogmatic system is given in *Gl.* § 16: namely, scripture contains little language of the descriptively didactic type. But only descriptively didactic language may be used in dogmatic propositions.

12. *Gl.*, §§ 15, 19 (ET, 76–78, 88–93).

13. The most important treatments of Schleiermacher's sermons are the following: Karl Barth, *Die Theologie Schleiermachers: Vorlesungen Göttingen Wintersemester 1923/24*, ed. Dietrich Ritschl (Zurich: Theologischer Verlag, 1978); Johannes Bauer, *Schleiermacher als patriotischer Prediger* (Giessen: Töpelmann, 1908); Wolfgang Trillhaas, *Schleiermachers Predigt und das homiletische Problem*, 2d ed. (Berlin: Walter de Gruyter, 1975); Christoph Meier-Dörken, *Die Theologie der frühen Predigten Schleiermachers* (Berlin: Walter de Gruyter, 1988). Fortunately, the sermons are now receiving more attention. An entire section of the 1984 Schleiermacher Congress in Berlin was devoted to the theme: "Schleiermacher as an Exegete and

Preacher." For the essays generated by this section, see *Internationaler Schleiermacher-Kongress Berlin 1984*, ed. Kurt-Victor Selge, Schleiermacher Archiv, I.i-ii (Berlin: Walter de Gruyter, 1985), 643–770. See also K. G. Jung, *Der Erlösungsbegriff der frühen Predigten F. D. E. Schleiermachers* (Berlin University thesis, 1971); F. Krotz, *Predigt und Glaube: F. Schleiermacher über Christi Liebe* (Marburg University thesis, 1974).

14. Barth, *Das Wort Gottes und die Theologie*, 164.

15. See the interesting collection of essays in James O. Duke and Robert F. Streetman, eds., *Barth and Schleiermacher: Beyond the Impasse?* (Philadelphia: Fortress Press, 1988). See also Martin Ohst, *Schleiermacher und die Bekenntnisschriften: Eine Untersuchung zu seiner Reformations- und Protestantismusdeutung*, Beiträge zur Historischen Theologie, 77 (Tübingen: J.C.B. Mohr [Paul Siebeck], 1989).

16. The epigraphs to this chapter point to one such formal similarity between Calvin and Schleiermacher. (Calvin, *Comm. 2 Tim.* 3:15 [CO 52:382]; Schleiermacher, *Hermeneutik, nach den Handschriften neu herausgegeben und eingeleitet*, ed. Heinz Kimmerle [Heidelberg: Carl Winter, 1959], 43.)

17. Barth's interpretation of Schleiermacher cannot be found in one text alone—it spans his entire career as a theologian, and it would not be incorrect to say that his ongoing struggle with Schleiermacher had much to do with Barth's self-understanding as a theologian. He lectured on the theology of Schleiermacher during his first years of teaching at Göttingen University and these lectures were published posthumously. (*Die Theologie Schleiermachers: Vorlesungen Göttingen Wintersemester 1923/24*, ed. Dietrich Ritschl [Zurich: Theologischer Verlag, 1978]; ET, *The Theology of Schleiermacher: Lectures at Göttingen, Winter Semester 1923/24*, ed. Dietrich Ritschl, trans. Geoffrey W. Bromiley [Grand Rapids: Wm. B. Eerdmans Publishing Co., 1982]). The "Concluding Unscientific Postscript" is a piece Barth contributed as an afterword to an edition of selected Schleiermacher works ("Nachwort," in *Schleiermacher Auswahl*, ed. H. Bolli [Munich and Hamburg: Siebenstern Taschenbuch Verlag, 1968]; ET in *The Theology of Schleiermacher*). Barth's understanding of Schleiermacher, while consistent for the most part, is also a complicated subject in its own right. See Dietmar Lütz, *Homo Viator: Karl Barths Ringen mit Schleiermacher* (Zurich: Theologischer Verlag, 1988), esp. 359–400. A thoroughgoing estimation of Barth's relationship to Schleiermacher has yet to be written.

18. Barth, *The Theology of Schleiermacher*, 210.

19. Ibid., 205.

20. For a detailed demonstration of this point, see E.H.U. Quapp, *Barth contra Schleiermacher: "Die Weihnachtsfeier" als Nagelprobe* (Marburg: Karl Wenzel, 1978).

21. In his essay on "The Need and Promise of Christian Preaching," Barth writes: "The Reformation wished to see something better substituted for the mass it abolished . . . our preaching of the Word. For the *verbum visibile*, the objectively clarified preaching of the Word, is the only sacrament left to us" (*Das Wort Gottes und die Theologie*, 110).

22. *The Eclipse of the Biblical Narrative: A Study in Eighteenth and Nineteenth Century Hermeneutics* (New Haven, Conn.: Yale University Press, 1974), 10.

23. Ibid., 2–3.

24. Ibid., 18–37.

25. Ibid., 23.

26. Ibid., 37.

27. Ibid., 300–324.

28. Ibid., 313.

29. George W. Stroup makes this point, although he comes to a different conclusion than I do, in his essay "Narrative in Calvin's Hermeneutic," in *John Calvin and the Church: A Prism of Reform*, ed. Timothy George (Louisville, Ky.: Westminster/John Knox Press, 1990), 163–65, 168.

30. Cf. William J. Bouwsma, *John Calvin: A Sixteenth Century Portrait* (New York and Oxford: Oxford University Press, 1988), 124–25.

31. For Calvin's view of the relationship between preaching and biblical interpretation, see Dieter Schellong, *Calvins Auslegung der synoptischen Evangelien* (Munich: Chr. Kaiser Verlag, 1969), 34–42. For Schleiermacher's understanding of preaching, see the introduction in *Servant of the Word: Selected Sermons of Friedrich Schleiermacher*, trans. and ed. Dawn DeVries (Philadelphia: Fortress Press, 1987), 5–12; for Schleiermacher's view of the task of exegesis, see his *KD*, §§ 103–48.

32. David Friedrich Strauss, *Der Christus des Glaubens und der Jesus der Geschichte: Eine Kritik des Schleiermacher'schen Lebens Jesu* (Berlin, 1865); reprint ed., ed. Hans-Jürgen Geischer, Texte zur Kirchen- und Theologiegeschichte, vol. 14 (Gütersloher Verlagshaus Gerd Mohn, 1971), 106. (ET, *The Christ of Faith and the Jesus of History: A Critique of Schleiermacher's Life of Jesus*, trans. and ed. Leander E. Keck [Philadelphia: Fortress Press, 1977], 169.)

33. Richard R. Niebuhr argues that the term "christomorphic" is a more adequate description of the character of the *Glaubenslehre* than "christocentric," since Schleiermacher does not deduce everything else in his system from Christology (*Schleiermacher on Christ and Religion* [London: SCM Press, 1964], 210–14).

34. That is, does the substitutionary atonement of Christ that Calvin seems to favor in Book 2 actually accomplish salvation, or does it merely open up the possibility of a salvation to be accomplished later, when the believer unites with Christ? Calvin's own comments at the opening of Book 3 seem to suggest the latter answer: "As long as Christ remains outside of us, and we are separated from him, all that he has suffered and done for the salvation of the human race remains useless" (*Inst.*, 3.1.1 [ET, 1:537]). On this tension in Calvin's system, cf. Paul van Buren, *Christ in Our Place: The Substitutionary Character of Calvin's Doctrine of Reconciliation* (Edinburgh: Oliver & Boyd, 1957), 32; B. A. Gerrish, "Atonement and 'Saving Faith,'" *Theology Today* 17 (July 1960): 184.

35. D. F. Strauss's ruthless critique of Schleiermacher's position remains valid. See his *Leben Jesu*, 710–20 (ET, 768–73).

36. F.D.E. Schleiermacher, *Das Leben Jesu: Vorlesungen an der Universität zu Berlin im Jahr 1832*, ed. K. A. Rütenik (Berlin: Reimer, 1864); in Schleiermacher's *Sämmtliche Werke*, 30 vols. in three parts (Berlin: Reimer, 1834–64), I/6:22–29. Hereafter cited as SW.

# 2

# CALVIN ON THE
# WORD AS SACRAMENT

I take it for granted that there is such life energy in God's Word that it
quickens the souls of all to whom God grants participation in it.
*Institutes of the Christian Religion*

For we know that justification is lodged in Christ alone and that it is
communicated to us no less by the preaching of the gospel than by the
seal of the sacrament. . . . Therefore, let it be regarded as a settled principle that the sacraments have the same office as the Word of God: to
offer and set forth Christ to us, and in him the treasures of heavenly
grace.
*Short Treatise on the Lord's Supper*

Calvin, like Luther before him, borrowed from Augustine the notion that
sacraments were "visible words."[1] While this meant that the Reformers
tended to verbalize the sacraments, it also led them to "sacramentalize"
the Word.[2] In order to understand the significance of Calvin's doctrine of
the Word, however, we must first explore how preaching was understood
by Calvin's predecessors.

## THE DOCTRINE OF THE WORD AND THE TASK
## OF PREACHING BEFORE CALVIN

While it cannot be asserted that the Reformers of the sixteenth century
invented the notion of the Word as a means of grace, it is commonly said
that they raised the discussion to a wholly new level.[3] Already in Origen
one can discover an appreciation for the importance of the preaching of
the Word in the life of the faithful.[4] But in Augustine's writings against the
Donatists, the parallelism of Word and sacrament first receives explicit
statement.[5] Both Word and sacraments are instruments for communicating the grace by which God justifies and sanctifies the elect: the Word is
the seed of regeneration.

At the same time, however, Augustine also understood the Word as a
means of instruction for the faithful. And it is the didactic understanding
of the Word that came to prevail in the Middle Ages, when, increasingly,
the infusion of grace was taken to be the special office of the sacraments
of Baptism and Eucharist. The preached Word was a means of teaching,
communicating the truth, and preparing people to receive the sacraments.
But it was only the *preparation for*, and not the instrument of communicating, the grace of salvation.[6]

This preparation should consist in two things: catechetical instruction and moral urging. The average churchgoer in the Middle Ages was not well instructed in the rudiments of the faith. If he or she knew how to say the Lord's Prayer, or the Ave Maria, for example, he or she was considered remarkably educated. Much medieval preaching, then, simply tried to convey the words of prayers and creeds, and their meaning, to the hearers of sermons.[7] At the same time, however, medieval preachers tried to stimulate in their hearers the desire to receive the church's sacraments by stressing the demands of the moral law, the fleetingness of life, and the terrors of hell.[8] The preached Word itself, so far from conveying the healing medicine of divine grace, was rather a prescription for the medicine that was available only in the sacraments.

By the end of the Middle Ages, this conception of preaching was beginning to come undone. Even before Luther and the first generation of Protestant reformers, the Augustinian notion of the Word as a means of grace was being recovered.[9] But Luther went farther: he took Romans 10:17 as a radical principle for reform. Faith comes from hearing; thus, the grace of God is infused primarily through the preaching of the Word, and only secondarily through the sacraments.[10] Even the life of Jesus is interpreted through the lens of the sacramental Word. Luther states:

> If I had to do without one or the other,—either the works or preaching of Christ,—I would rather do without His works than His preaching; for the works do not help me, but His words give life, as He Himself says. Now John writes very little about the works of Christ, but very much about His preaching, while the other Evangelists write much of His works and little of His preaching; therefore John's Gospel is the one, tender, true chief Gospel, far, far to be preferred to the other three and placed high above them. So, too, the Epistles of St. Paul and St. Peter far surpass the other three Gospels,—Matthew, Mark and Luke.[11]

Calvin, then, was following an old and established tradition—freshly appropriated in the sixteenth century—in understanding the Word as the primary means of grace to which the sacraments are but "appendages."[12] But now we must ask what precisely Calvin meant by "the Word."

## THE WORD OF GOD: SCRIPTURE, PREACHING, AND THE INCARNATION

Calvin's use of the term "Word of God" is ambiguous at best. It is often unclear to what exactly the "Word" refers.[13] Certainly Calvin wishes to maintain that the Word of God is found reliably in scripture. But Calvin does not simply equate the words of scripture with the Word of God.[14]

For, as he puts it in his commentary on 2 Timothy 3:15, "False prophets also make use of it [scripture] as a pretext; and so, in order that it may be useful to us for salvation, we have to know how to use it rightly."[15] The correct use of scripture involves seeking in it what we need to know for our salvation—or, more correctly, *whom* we need to know, namely, Jesus Christ. Thus, the center of scripture, its unifying purpose, is to present Christ and his saving work to those who are to be saved.[16]

One of Calvin's favorite shorthand terms for the center of scripture is "gospel." The gospel is "an embassy [*legatio*], by which the reconciliation of the world with God, once for all accomplished in the death of Christ, is daily conveyed to men."[17] The gospel, in other words, is not only the announcement, but the actual gift imparting God's promised grace. It communicates or presents Christ to its hearers, and unites them to God through Christ. In fact, Calvin goes so far as to say that the gospel itself *brings* salvation.[18] In presenting Christ, the gospel reveals the fatherly goodwill of God, and so enables the hearers of the Word, if God wills, to receive the gifts of justification and sanctification.[19]

Calvin is very clear, however, that the gospel comes to us, or communicates Christ to us, only in the proclaimed Word of preaching and sacraments.[20] Private reading of and meditation on scripture is not sufficient. In a fascinating passage in his *Commentary on John* (Jesus' reference to the story of Moses' lifting the brazen serpent over the people in 3:14), Calvin argues explicitly that the preaching of the gospel is to be understood sacramentally.

> To be lifted up means to be set in a lofty and eminent place, so as to be exhibited to the view of all. This was done by the preaching of the gospel; for the explanation of it which some give, as referring to the cross, neither agrees with the context nor is applicable to the present subject. The simple meaning of the words, therefore, is that by the preaching of the gospel, Christ would be raised on high. . . . Christ introduces [the illustration of the brazen serpent] in this passage, in order to show that he must be placed before the eyes of all by the teaching of the gospel, that all who look at him by faith may receive salvation. And so we ought to infer that Christ is clearly shown to us in the gospel . . . and that faith has its own faculty of vision, by which to perceive him as if present; as Paul tells us that a lively portrait of Christ with his cross is portrayed, when he is truly preached (Gal. 3:1). . . . A question now arises: Does Christ compare himself to the *serpent,* because there is some resemblance; or, does he pronounce it to have been a sacrament, as the Manna was? For though the Manna was bodily food, intended for present use, yet Paul testifies that it was a spiritual mystery (1 Cor. 10:3). I am led to think this was also the case with the brazen serpent.[21]

This passage is remarkable for several reasons. First, Calvin speaks of the preaching of the gospel as a kind of manifestation of Christ's presence.

"Faith has its own faculty of vision [*fidei adspectum*] by which to perceive Christ as if present." Thus, the gospel not only conveys information about, but also renders the veritable presence of, Jesus Christ. It is interesting that Calvin goes out of his way to deny the obvious interpretation of the text: that Jesus was alluding to his death on the cross. Even more remarkable, however, is the suggestion with which he concludes his comments on this verse: namely, that Jesus refers to the serpent because it was a sacrament. Calvin's understanding of the unity of the Old and New Testaments in one covenant of grace required that he discover in the Old Testament "types" of significant aspects of New Testament faith. Thus, with regard to the sacraments, circumcision is the Old Testament type of baptism.[22] It seems that in the passage above, Calvin is arguing that the brazen serpent was the Old Testament type of the New Testament sacrament of the Word—the preaching of the gospel. But Calvin is more certain that the Word is sacramental than he is that he has given the only possible interpretation of this passage in John: he concludes that "if anyone comes to a different opinion about this, I do not debate the point with him."[23]

The Word of God, then, refers first and foremost to Jesus Christ, the incarnate *Logos*, who secured the reconciliation of elect humanity with God. For present-day believers, an encounter with Christ the Word is possible when the words of scripture are truly preached and heard. Preaching under the power of the Holy Spirit focuses, as it were, the vision of believers on the center of scripture—Christ—and in that moment of insight, faith perceives the immediate presence of the Redeemer.[24] Thus preaching itself becomes the Word of God, in the sense that it discloses the person of Christ and Christ's witness to his Father.[25]

## THE FUNCTION OF THE SACRAMENTAL WORD

Calvin frequently states that the Word and the sacraments have the same purpose or office: to offer and present Christ.[26] Thus it should not surprise us that Calvin describes the function of the preached Word as analogous to the function of sacraments—both are instruments of divine grace.[27] He often speaks of preaching as a mirror in which we can behold the face of Christ and of God.[28] The Word in this sense reveals the gracious character of God and the love of the Savior. Yet Calvin is not satisfied with an understanding of the Word that could be merely educational and would appeal only to the cognitive faculties of human beings. Like the sacraments, preaching works, according to Calvin, in appealing to the entire person (not just the intellect) through an attractive picture. Preachers present Christ so forcefully that their hearers can "see" and "hear" Christ themselves as if he were confronting them directly.[29]

The verb Calvin frequently uses to describe the function of the sacramental Word is *exhibere:* to present or represent.[30] The Word and the sacraments are exhibitive signs—they present or offer what they represent. Calvin explicitly rejects a merely memorialistic understanding of representation, that is, that the sacraments are like pictures that remind the partakers of things they represent.[31] On the contrary, the sacraments themselves confer grace. Calvin explains that by "exhibit" he means nothing less than to *give*.[32]

As in his discussion of sacraments, Calvin explicitly denies that the Word is a *bare* sign—that is, a sign devoid of the reality it represents. The Word itself is efficacious—it brings what it portrays.[33] The gift of the Word is the presence of Christ with all the benefits that he has secured for the elect—specifically, the twofold grace of justification and sanctification.[34] In addition, the preaching of the Word is itself the true exercise of the keys of the kingdom: it has the power both to save and to damn.[35] Calvin even speaks of preaching as "ratifying" the salvation secured in Christ's death.[36]

God uses the instrument of the Word, however, in such a way that its power and efficacy remain God's own. Calvin is careful to avoid what he takes to be the mechanistic implications of the Roman Catholic view that sacraments function *ex opere operato*.[37] Only when the Word is effectively sealed by the Holy Spirit can it be said to offer and present Christ to us. And if Calvin reserves the possibility that God can work faith in the hearts of the elect quite apart from any outward signs, he also insists that God is not bound to communicate grace only through the Word.[38] Nonetheless, Calvin is quick to insist that preaching, like the sacraments, is the regular and ordinary means by which God chooses to communicate the benefit of Christ's work.[39]

Both Word and sacraments are "accommodations" to human weakness. God "provides for our weakness in that he prefers to address us in human fashion through interpreters in order to draw us to himself, rather than to thunder at us and drive us away."[40] Likewise, since we are "creatures who always creep on the ground . . . he condescends to lead us to himself even by these earthly elements, and to set before us in the flesh a mirror of spiritual blessings."[41] Some people, Calvin says, have difficulty accepting such accommodations. They believe God's Word is "dragged down by the baseness of the men called to teach it" and that they could benefit just as much from private meditation on the scripture.[42] They believe it improbable that a "drop of water" suffices to assure us of remission of sins, or that "a piece of bread and a drop of wine suffice to assure us that God accepts us as his children" and that in them we receive Jesus Christ and all his benefits.[43] Such doubts are understandable in respect to the true lowliness of the instruments consecrated to God's use, but they do not excuse believers from the necessity of acknowledging God's presence in the events of preaching and sacraments.

Calvin offers several explanations for why God chooses to work through all too fallible human instruments. First, the human mediation of the Word is an exercise in humility. If God were to speak to us directly from heaven, everyone would hear and believe, because everyone would be terrified at the majesty of God's glory. "But when a puny man risen up from the dust speaks in God's name, at this point we best evidence our piety and obedience toward God if we show ourselves teachable toward his minister, although he excels us in nothing."[44] Second, the ministry provides "the chief sinew by which believers are held together in one body."[45] If individuals were allowed to interpret scripture for themselves in isolation, each would despise the other, and there would be as many churches as there are individuals.

Ultimately, however, the use of human mediation for the Word is, like the incarnation itself, part of the mystery of divine grace in salvation. For the incarnation itself was also an accommodation to human weakness. Christ, the Mediator, was known to the patriarchs under the law. And the work of the Mediator was the same in the Old Covenant as it is in the New: to reveal the parental goodwill of God toward the elect.[46] But in emptying himself and taking on human flesh, the Mediator assures us, in the weakness of our conscience, that he is approachable—that we need not be afraid to come to him for help. Indeed, it is Christ who has come to *us* and extends his hand to us. As Calvin says in his commentary on Hebrews:

> It was not, indeed, the Apostle's object to weary us with . . . subtleties . . . but only to teach us that we have not to go far to seek a Mediator, since Christ of his own accord extends his hand to us, that we have no reason to dread the majesty of Christ since he is our brother, and that there is no cause to fear, lest he, as one unacquainted with evils, should not be touched by any feeling of humanity, so as to bring us help, since he took upon him our infirmities in order that he might be more inclined to succor us. . . . And the chief benefit of . . . [this] is a sure confidence in calling on God, as, on the other hand, the whole of religion falls to the ground, and is lost, when this certainty is taken away from consciences.[47]

This work of restoring human confidence in the goodness of God is carried on through the proclamation of the gospel. For Christ's own office of proclaiming the name of God and of filling all things is fulfilled in the ministry.[48] Thus the preached Word not only conveys Christ, but also continues Christ's living presence in the world. The sacramental Word is a re-presentation of the person and work of Christ. In this sense, the Word itself gives life and salvation, for it enables the hearers to receive the benefit of Christ's reconciling work.[49]

## THE SACRAMENTAL WORD AND
## THE TASK OF MINISTRY

If the preaching of the gospel is the very continuation of the presence of Christ in the world, it should not surprise us that for Calvin, and the Reformed tradition after him, the sermon takes on a liturgical significance not unlike that of the Eucharist itself. Calvin insisted that Word and sacrament must never be separated. He could not imagine a Eucharist without the proclamation of the gospel in preaching. But neither did he believe that preaching alone, without a celebration of the Eucharist, was sufficient for regular worship. He argued for years with the magistrates of the city of Geneva, trying to convince them of the importance of weekly Communion. But finally he compromised and agreed to a quarterly celebration of Communion (even though he was preaching almost daily). From that time on, churches in the Reformed tradition tended to elevate preaching to a position of relatively greater importance than that of the sacraments.[50]

There is a certain ambivalence to this emphasis on the Word. On the one hand, Reformed worship can be aridly intellectual and devoid of the mystical element that always remained a part of Calvin's piety.[51] And Reformed ministers—perhaps even Calvin himself—sometimes appear to arrogate to themselves inordinate authority because of their office of proclaiming God's Word to the church. On the other hand, however, the Reformed theology of the Word captures the scandal of particularity that is the scandal of incarnation itself: the Word of God comes in the form of human flesh.

It can hardly be overemphasized what a paradigm shift this understanding of the Word represented in sixteenth-century theology. Grace was no longer an incrementally infused quality but renewed personal relationship, made possible by God's initiative in addressing sinners.[52] The Roman Church, in the Council of Trent, decisively rejected this concept of grace. While they recognized the necessity of preaching and reading the Bible, the Tridentine fathers never attributed to preaching the function of conveying grace. The reference to Romans 10:17 in the "Decree Concerning Justification" falls in a chapter on *preparation* for receiving grace.[53] Like their medieval predecessors, the theologians at Trent could not see preaching as anything more than a preparation for receiving the sacraments "through which all true justice either begins, or being begun is increased, or being lost is restored."[54]

For Calvin, on the contrary, the one thing necessary is the Word that offers and presents Christ; without this Word, the sacraments are nothing more than vain superstitions.[55] But how can the preacher do this? How must sermons be constructed in order to be effective means of grace? Calvin never wrote a technical treatise on homiletics, and so we must look at his own preaching practice for answers to these questions. It is to this task that we turn in the next chapter.

## NOTES

1. *Inst.*, 4.14.6 (ET, 2:1281). Augustine, *In Joannis Evangelium Tractatus*, lxxx.3 (J. P. Migne, ed., *Patrologiae cursus completus, series Latina*, 221 vols. [Paris, 1844–1900], 35.1840).

2. T.H.L. Parker describes this feature of Calvin's doctrine of preaching in his *The Oracles of God: An Introduction to the Preaching of John Calvin* (London: Lutterworth, 1947), 53–56. Ernst Bizer notes the same characteristic in Luther's theology in his important study *Fides ex auditu: Eine Untersuchung über die Entdeckung der Gerechtigkeit Gottes durch Martin Luther* (Neukirchen: Verlag der Buchhandlung des Erziehungsvereins, 1958), 160. Others have referred to the sacramental Word in Calvin's theology. See B. A. Gerrish, "The Reformers' Theology of Worship," *McCormick Quarterly* 14 (1961): 29; Richard Stauffer, "Le Discours à la première personne dans les sermons de Calvin," in *Regards contemporains sur Jean Calvin* (Paris, 1965); Georges Bavaud, "Les Rapports entre la prédication et les sacrements dans le contexte du dialogue oecuménique," in *Communion et communication: Structures d'unité et modèles de communication de l'évangile. Troisième Cycle romand en théologie practique (1976–77)* (Geneva: Labor et Fides, 1978), 69–73; B. A. Gerrish, *The Old Protestantism and the New: Essays on the Reformation Heritage* (Chicago: University of Chicago Press, 1982), 106–17; John H. Leith, "Calvin's Doctrine of the Proclamation of the Word and Its Significance for Today," in *John Calvin and the Church: A Prism of Reform*, ed. Timothy George (Louisville, Ky.: Westminster/John Knox Press, 1990), 211–12, 219; B. A. Gerrish, *Grace and Gratitude: The Eucharistic Theology of John Calvin* (Minneapolis: Augsburg Fortress Press, 1992), 82–86.

3. See the articles, "Predigt," and "Wort Gottes," in *Die Religion in Geschichte und Gegenwart*, 3d ed., ed. Hans von Campenhausen et al., 6 vols. (Tübingen: J.C.B. Mohr [Paul Siebeck], 1957–62), 5:516–39, 6:1809–21. Cf. the article "Preaching," in *The New Schaff-Herzog Encyclopedia of Religious Knowledge*, ed. Samuel Macauley Jackson et al., 12 vols. (New York and London: Funk & Wagnalls, 1908–14), 9:158–89.

4. Jean Daniélou, *Origen*, trans. W. Mitchell (New York: Sheed & Ward, 1955), 65.

5. As Harnack notes, "To begin with it was an immense advance, only possible to so spiritual a man as Augustine, to rank the Word along with the Sacraments. It is to him we owe the phrase 'the Word and the Sacraments.' If he did not duly appreciate and carry out the import of the 'Word,' yet he perceived that as gospel it lay at the root of every saving rite of the church" (Adolf von Harnack, *History of Dogma*, trans. from the 3d German ed. by Neil Buchanan, 7 vols. [London, 1900; reprint, Gloucester, Mass.: Peter Smith, 1976], 5:155). Cf. Reinhold

Seeberg, *Textbook of the History of Doctrines*, trans. Charles E. Hay, 2 vols. (Grand Rapids: Baker Book House, 1952), 2:282. See also Richard H. Grützmacher, *Wort und Geist: Eine historische und dogmatische Untersuchung zum Gnadenmittel des Wortes* (Leipzig: A. Deichert'sche Verlagsbuchhandlung [Georg Böhme], 1902), 1–7.

6. Grützmacher attributes the increasing emphasis on the didactic character of the Word to the intensification of Augustine's predestinarianism in his later years and the corresponding need he felt to distinguish sharply between the inner work of the Spirit and the outer Word of preaching (*Wort und Geist*, 1–7). But in addition it should be noted that the Augustinian doctrine of sin and redemption created the need for a system of penance and satisfaction that rendered the Word as such less important for growth in grace.

7. See T.H.L. Parker, *The Oracles of God*, 13–21; cf. Elmer Carl Kiessling, *The Early Sermons of Luther and Their Relation to the Pre-Reformation Sermon* (Grand Rapids: Zondervan Publishing House, 1935), 9–41; cf. also the articles on "Preaching," in *New Catholic Encyclopedia*, vol. 11 (New York: McGraw-Hill Book Co., 1967), 684–702. Of course the preaching theory and practice of the Middle Ages is a complex subject in its own right, and the paragraphs above are not intended to serve as anything more than a simple background to the discussion of Calvin's understanding of preaching that follows.

8. See Michel Zink, *La Prédication en Langue Romane avant 1300* (Paris: Editions Honoré Champion, 1976), 431–75.

9. For example, the Strassburg preacher John Geiler of Keisersberg (1445–1510) seems to have understood preaching as a means of grace (E. Jane Dempsey Douglass, *Justification in Late Medieval Preaching: A Study of John Geiler of Keisersberg*, 2d ed. [Leiden: E. J. Brill, 1989], 82–91).

10. See Ernst Bizer, *Fides ex auditu*. Harnack states: "Luther reduced the sacraments . . . to one only, namely, the Word of God. . . . For Luther . . . the sacraments are really only the 'visible word' . . . but the Word which is strong and mighty, because in it God himself works upon us and transacts with us. In the last analysis, it is a contrariety in the view of grace that comes out with special directness here. According to the Catholic view, grace is the power that is applied and infused through the sacraments, which, on condition of the cooperation of free will, enables man to fulfill the law of God and to acquire the merits that are requisite for salvation. But according to Luther grace is the Fatherly disposition of God, calling guilty man for Christ's sake to himself and receiving him by winning his trust through the presentation of the picture of Christ" (Harnack, *History of Dogma*, 7:216–17); cf. Seeberg, "Medieval theology constructed the doctrine of the sacraments. Luther was the first to frame a doctrine of the Word of God" (Seeberg, *Textbook of the History of Doctrines*, 2:282).

11. Martin Luther, *Preface to the New Testament* (1545 [1522]), in *Luther's Works*, ed. Jaroslav Pelikan and Helmut T. Lehmann, 55 vols. (St. Louis: Concordia Publishing House; Philadelphia: Fortress Press, 1955-76), 6:443–44. This statement could have been made *verbatim* by F.D.E. Schleiermacher some three hundred years later. See chapter 4 below. One can find many more references to the Word as sacrament in Luther's works. See, for example, his sermon for Christmas Day 1519: "All the words and all the narratives of the Gospel are a kind of sacraments: that is, sacred signs by which God effects in believers what the narratives signify"

(D. Martin Luthers Werke: Kritische Gesamtausgabe [Weimar, 1883–], 9.440.3; hereafter cited as WA). In his 1519 Commentary on Galatians Luther states, "The Word,
I say, and the Word alone is the vehicle of divine grace" (WA 2.509.13).
    12. Inst., 4.14.3, 14 (ET, 2:1278, 1289–90). It must be noted, however, that Luther
and Calvin do not understand the sacramental Word in precisely the same way.
In fact, their respective views on preaching mirror their different understandings
of the sacraments. See T.H.L. Parker, The Oracles of God, 45ff.
    13. For an excellent discussion of this problem, see John T. McNeill, "The Sig-
nificance of the Word of God for Calvin," Church History 28 (1959): 131–46, esp. 139.
    14. Inst., 1.7–9 (ET, 1:74–96). See also B. A. Gerrish, The Old Protestantism and the
New, 58–64, 296–300; Alexandre Ganoczy and Stefan Scheld, Die Hermeneutik
Calvins: Geistesgeschichtliche Voraussetzungen und Grundzüge, Veröffentlichungen
des Instituts für Europäische Geschichte Mainz, vol. 114 (Wiesbaden: Franz
Steiner Verlag, 1983), 90–92; H. Jackson Forstman, Word and Spirit: Calvin's Doc-
trine of Biblical Authority (Stanford, Calif.: Stanford University Press, 1962).
    15. Comm. 2 Tim. 3:15 (CO 52:382).
    16. See, for example, his preface to Olivetán's New Testament (CO 9:815) and
Comm. John 5:39 (CO 47:125). For more discussion of the limits of Calvin's bibli-
cism, see B. A. Gerrish, The Old Protestantism and the New, 61–62, and H. Jackson
Forstman, Word and Spirit, 39–41.
    17. Comm. Harm. of the Gospel (CO 45:1).
    18. Comm. Gal. 1:7 (CO 50:173); Comm. 1 Peter 1:13 (CO 55:221); Comm. Titus 1:3
(CO 52:407); Comm. 1 John 1:3 (CO 55:302), Comm. Acts 5:20 (CO 48:106–7); Comm.
Eph. 3:7 (CO 51:180).
    19. Comm. Eph. 2:17 (CO 51:173).
    20. See, for example, Comm. Rom. 1:16; 16:21 (CO 49:19, 290); and Comm. Titus
1:3 (CO 52:407). It is quite appropriate to take preaching as the primary sense in
which Calvin used the term "Word of God," since he almost always translated verbum Dei as "la Parole de Dieu," a term that is used only for the spoken, not the written, word. In this matter, however, Calvin was not original. Erasmus before him,
in his Latin translation of the New Testament, had rendered John 1:1 as "In the beginning was the speech [sermo]" (Un inédit d'Erasme: La première version du Nouveau
Testament: copiée par Pierre Meghen, 1506–1509, ed. Henri Gibaud [Angers: H.
Gibaud, 1982], 188).
    21. Comm. John 3:14 (CO 47:62–63). It is interesting that Calvin gives essentially
the same explanation of this event and Jesus' reference to it when he comments on
the Old Testament passage that originally recounts it (Comm. Num. 21:8–9 [CO
25:249–50]). Schleiermacher argues in a similar fashion that, "if one understands
the 'lifting up' to refer to the crucifixion of Christ, that is a totally capricious interpretation; nothing more is meant by 'lifting up' than to become generally visible"
(Das Leben Jesu [SW I/6:345]). Calvin speaks of Christ "as if" present, in this passage, not to deny the real presence of Christ, but to distinguish his spiritual presence from a crassly physical or local presence. This is exactly the same move Calvin
makes when speaking of the presence of Christ in the Lord's Supper. See B. A. Gerrish, Grace and Gratitude, 145n, 180–81n.
    22. Inst., 2.9–11, 4.14.18–26 (ET, 1:423–64, 2:1294–1303).
    23. Comm. John 3:14 (CO 47:63).
    24. Comm. John 7:33 (CO 47:178).

25. This understanding of the preaching event was taken up into the Reformed tradition and preserved in the *Second Helvetic Confession* (1566), written by the Zurich reformer Heinrich Bullinger (1504–66). It states: "Proinde cum hodie hoc Dei verbum per praedicatores legitime vocatos annunciatur in Ecclesia, credimus ipsum Dei verbum annunciari et a fidelibus recipi, neque aliud Dei verbum vel fingendum, vel coelitus esse exspectandum" (*The Creeds of Christendom,* ed. Philip Schaff [New York: Harper, 1877; 4th ed., 1919], vol. 3, 237).

26. The second passage I used for an epigraph to this chapter states this clearly (*Petit traicté de la Saincte Cene de nostre Seigneur Iesus Christ* [CO 5:435]).

27. *Inst.,* 2.5.5, 4.14.12 (ET, 1:321–23, 2:1287); *Comm. Acts* 16:14 (CO 48:378); *Comm. Eph.* 5:26 (CO 51:223–24).

28. See sermon 31 on the harmony of the Gospels (CO 46:378); see also *Comm. Matt.* 4:1 (CO 45:128); *Comm. Luke* 2:30 (CO 45:90); *Comm. John* 3:14 (CO 47:62–63); *Comm. John* 8:19 (CO 47:195); *Comm. 1 Peter* 1:13 (CO 55:221).

29. *Comm. Isa.* 11:4 (CO 36:240); *Comm. Gal.* 3:1 (CO 50:202–3).

30. For example in *Inst.,* 1.9.3 (ET, 1:95–96); cf. the argument to the sermons on the Harmony of the Gospels (CO 46:v).

31. This was Zwingli's understanding of the sacraments. For Calvin's criticism of it, see his letter to Heinrich Bullinger, February 25, 1547 (CO 12:480–89).

32. CO 12:483–88.

33. *Inst.,* 4.17.5, 10 (ET, 2:1364–65, 1370–71); *Comm. John* 1:12 (CO 47:12); *Comm. John* 6:51 (CO 47:153); *Comm. Heb.* 4:2, 12 (CO 55:45–46, 49–52); *Comm. 1 Peter* 1:23, 25 (CO 55:228–31); *Comm. 1 John* 1:1–2 (CO 55:301–2).

34. *Petit traicté de la Saincte Cene* (CO 5:435); *Comm. John* 15:3, 17:17 (CO 47:340, 385); *Comm. Acts* 5:20, 10:36 (CO 48:106–7, 244).

35. *Inst.,* 4.1.22 (ET, 2:1035–36); cf. *Comm. Matt.* 3:12 (CO 45:123); *Comm. 1 Tim.* 4:16 (CO 52:303–4).

36. *Comm. Acts* 26:18 (CO 48:542); cf. *Comm. John* 20:23 (CO 47:441).

37. *Inst.,* 4.14.14 (ET, 2:1289–90); cf. *Comm. Acts* 7:35 (CO 48:149).

38. *Inst.,* 1.7, 1.8.3, 4.14.14, 17 (ET, 1:74–81, 83–84, 2:1289–90, 1292–94); *Comm. Acts* 16:14 (CO 48:378); *Comm. Eph.* 5:26 (CO 51:223–24).

39. *Comm. Rom.* 10:14, 11:14 (CO 49:205, 219).

40. *Inst.,* 4.1.5 (ET, 2:1016–20).

41. *Inst.,* 4.14.3 (ET, 2:1278).

42. *Inst.,* 4.1.5 (ET, 2:1016–20).

43. *Serm. Luke 2:1–14* (CO 46:960).

44. *Inst.,* 4.3.1 (ET, 2:1054).

45. *Inst.,* 4.3.2 (ET, 2:1055).

46. *Inst.,* 2.6.2–4 (ET, 1:342–48).

47. *Comm. Heb.* 4:15–16 (CO 55:54–56).

48. *Inst.,* 4.3.2 (ET, 2:1054–55); *Comm. Heb.* 2:11 (CO 55:29).

49. The first epigraph I chose for this chapter conveys just this point (*Inst.,* 2.10.7 [ET, 1:434]).

50. William D. Maxwell, *An Outline of Christian Worship: Its Development and Forms* (London: Oxford University Press, 1936), 112–19.

51. In trying to explain the nature of Christ's presence in the sacrament of the Lord's Supper, Calvin states that "I experience rather than understand it" (*Inst.,* 4.17.32 [ET, 2:1403]).

52. See Melanchthon's discussion of grace in his *Loci Communes Theologici,* in *Melanchthon and Bucer,* Library of Christian Classics, vol. 19, ed. Wilhelm Pauck (Philadelphia: Westminster Press, 1969), 86–88.

53. *Canons and Decrees of the Council of Trent: Original Text with an English Translation,* trans. H. J. Schroeder, O.P. (St. Louis: B. Herder Books, 1941), 26, 32, 305, 311.

54. *Canons and Decrees of the Council of Trent,* 51, 329.

55. *Inst.,* 4.14.3–4 (ET, 2:1278–80).

# 3

# CALVIN'S SERMONS
# ON THE SYNOPTIC GOSPELS

Let those who would discharge aright the ministry of the gospel learn
not merely to speak and declaim, but to penetrate into the consciences
of men, to make them see Christ crucified, and feel the shedding of his
blood. When the church has painters such as these, it no longer needs
the dead images of wood and stone, it no longer requires pictures.

*Commentary on Galatians*, 3:1

As often as Christ calls us to the hope of salvation by the preaching of
the gospel, he is present with us. For not without reason is the preaching of the gospel called Christ's descent to us.

*Commentary on John*, 7:33

Given Calvin's Christocentric understanding of scripture, it is remarkable that he did not get around to preaching a series of sermons on the narratives about Jesus' life until very near the end of his career. The series of
sermons on the harmony of the Gospels began in summer of 1559 and
ended with Calvin's death in 1564.[1] This can, perhaps, be explained by the
fact that Calvin had completed his commentary on the harmony of the
Gospels only a few years before, in 1555.[2] Presumably, he was able to treat
most of the text of the Gospels in the five years in which he preached on
them. But, unfortunately, only a small number of these sermons are preserved in the *Calvini opera*. The editors published only those sermons
which had appeared in print during Calvin's lifetime: namely, sixty-five
sermons that cover Matthew 1–5:12, Mark 1, and Luke 1—4, and nine sermons on the history of the Passion and resurrection.[3] In what follows,
then, we shall discuss the way in which Calvin handles the Gospel history
with regard to three periods of Christ's life: before his baptism, during his
public ministry, and from his arrest to his resurrection. However, the emphasis will fall on the first and the last periods, since this is where we have
the most source material. This is not, however, out of line with Calvin's
own understanding of the life of Jesus. In his Geneva Catechism, the question is asked, "Why do you leap at once from his birth to his death, pass-
ing over the whole history of his life?" and the answer given is, "Because
nothing is treated of here but what so properly belongs to our salvation,
as in a manner to contain the substance of it."[4]

Calvin's preaching is expository: he simply reads the text and then
comments on it, verse by verse, noting both the exegesis and the application of each individual part.[5] This presents some difficulties for describing
the content of his sermons. Without an outline and its development, it is
difficult to summarize a sermon. For this reason, I have chosen sometimes

to analyze individual sermons extensively, in order to demonstrate Calvin's style of preaching and to indicate the full scope of his exposition; at other times, I have gathered evidence from several sermons that demonstrate a particular strategy of interpretation. We shall find that Calvin shows a perhaps surprising indifference to the narratives as narratives. Rather, he looks constantly for the "doctrine" they convey and, at the same time, perceives them as the means by which Christ makes himself present in Calvin's own day.

## SERMONS ON JESUS' LIFE
## BEFORE HIS BAPTISM

Of the sixty-five sermons on the harmony of the Gospels contained in the *Calvini opera*, thirty-nine deal with the period before Jesus' baptism. Not all of these, of course, will be equally interesting to us with respect to the question of how Calvin handles historical narratives. But before selecting a few sermons for special analysis, several general statements about this group as a whole need to be made.

One is struck in reading these sermons by the fact that Calvin rarely stays for long with the details of the narrative. Only when something seems at first glance problematic—difficult to understand—does he dwell on the actual words or events of the text itself. And even then he does not always busy himself with what is most pertinent to the story's meaning. Several examples may be offered. Calvin gives a long explanation of how Mary and Elizabeth could be cousins, since they are said to have come from different tribes of Israel: perhaps, he concludes, there is a conflating of maternal and paternal genealogies here.[6] He also offers an argument about the differences in the genealogies of Jesus in Matthew and Luke: the authors had different purposes in mind in composing their material.[7] He dwells on Matthew's choice of the word "virgin" for rendering Isaiah's prophecy about the birth of the Messiah: although Matthew did change the word, it was only to confirm the true meaning of the text, that is, that this was a miraculous sign. And, finally, he considers at some length the identity of the sages who visited the Holy Family in Bethlehem, the timing of their visit, and the kinds of gifts they may have brought.[8]

When he is not paying special attention to the actual words of the narrative, Calvin is usually doing one of two things. Either he is drawing out what he takes to be the meaning of the narrated events, and this is usually an item of doctrine, as we shall see; or he is applying or translating the text to a sixteenth-century context, often polemically, by arguing against the views of Roman Catholics, Lutherans, or others. I want now to give several illustrations of each technique.

It is, of course, easy to give poetic texts like the songs of Zechariah, Mary, and Simeon and the angelic pronouncements a doctrinal interpretation, and Calvin does so. The angel's announcement to Mary is a summary of the gospel.[9] His statement to Mary, "You have found favor," shows the true substance of joy: to be received into God's favor. We must remember, then, that every good thing proceeds from God's gratuitous goodwill.[10] It was important that the angel said explicitly that Mary would conceive in her womb. He wanted to show that the Savior was truly human and not just a phantasm or a ghost.[11]

Similarly, the Magnificat teaches us how God wants to be honored—namely, by the sacrifice of praise and thanksgiving that refers every good thing to its source in God. Mary's reference to her lowliness teaches us that we can properly praise God only when we recognize that we are nothing in ourselves. As Calvin proceeds in explicating the song of Mary, he finds in it many other doctrines, such as justification by faith alone and eternal election.[12]

Calvin almost always moves the discussion of poetic texts in a doctrinal direction. But what is more interesting for our purposes is that he reads the historical narratives in a similar way. Christ's birth in a stable is a symbol[13] of the humiliation of Christ in lowering himself to take our place before God's throne of judgment.[14] And the first announcement of the birth of Christ to vulgar shepherds is a symbol of God's choice of humble instruments for communicating the grace of the gospel.[15] The response of the people to the shepherds' message offers a lesson about the proper reception of the gospel.[16] And the sages came to see Jesus in order to demonstrate that the gospel is not incompatible with learning.[17]

Calvin does not always remain on the level of abstract doctrine. He also seeks to make the message of the text concrete in sixteenth-century terms. Sometimes this is done by a process of simple transference from the biblical situation to Calvin's own. In commenting on the angel's prediction to Zechariah that "you will have joy and gladness, and many will rejoice at his birth" (Luke 1:14), Calvin says that even though John is no longer alive, "we have this joy when the gospel is preached to us."[18] Similarly, Zechariah's incredulity at the message of the angel is like our anxiety and perplexity when we do not believe sufficiently in God's promise.[19] The disturbance Mary felt at the angel's greeting to her is like the fear we feel when contemplating God's majesty—a fear that predisposes us to receive God's Word.[20] And the scribes whom Herod consulted about the prophecies of the birth of the Messiah are like the bishops and prelates of the Roman Church (except that the scribes knew more about scripture).[21]

At other times, the transference leads Calvin into a prohibition or injunction. This is especially true of his polemical statements against the Church of Rome. The angel's announcement to Mary about the name of

Jesus is no justification for the papists' superstitious rites, such as genu-flecting to the altar.[22] We despoil God the Father and Jesus Christ of their honor if we call Mary the "Queen of Heaven" or our advocate. We would give Mary greater honor by following her example.[23] Thus, we also should know that we cannot use the Hail Mary as a prayer. These words of the angel were, in a sense, addressed to all God's children—us along with Mary. Only the statement "Blessed is the fruit of thy womb" is addressed specifically to Mary. For the rest, the words are a concise summary of the gospel.[24] Calvin similarly criticizes the practices of private baptism, prayer to the saints, the rite for the purification of women after childbirth, aspects of contemporary Mariology (Mary as a treasury of grace, the fes-tivals of the seven joys and woes), the glorification of celibacy, monastic vows, the use of icons in worship, and the practice of fasting.[25]

Calvin did not restrict his pulpit criticisms to the Church of Rome. On one occasion, in a long digression on the relation of Word and Eucharist, Calvin lashed out against the Lutherans, whose views on the subject, he states, are worse than those of the "Papists."[26] A particularly uncomfort-able application of the text appears at the end of his sermon on the song of Simeon. Calvin notes that the office (role or function) of the gospel is the same as that of Christ: to make plain what is hidden—chiefly our sins. The gospel portrays our sins before us like a portrait. Calvin then turns his ad-dress to two persons actually in the congregation before him who had de-nied the faith at the hands of Roman Catholic inquisitors, and he demands that they humble themselves before the church and ask for the prayers of the congregation.[27] And Calvin also criticized lingering relics of popular culture in Geneva, such as the celebration of St. John's fires.[28]

Clearly, the imperative mood was not reserved only for criticizing oth-ers, outside Calvin's congregation. His application of the text often chal-lenged his hearers themselves to a higher standard of behavior. The dilemma that Joseph faced in dealing with his pregnant fiancée should teach us how to deal with fellow believers caught in sin: to expose them simply to magnify their shame is inhumane.[29] The shepherds' mutual ex-hortation should teach us how to care for our salvation, each one helping and sustaining the other rather than going his or her own way selfishly.[30] And an attitude of humble reverence for God's Word, such as the shep-herds had, even when it appears contrary to reason, ought to characterize all Christians' attitudes toward scripture and preaching.[31]

Sometimes Calvin's contemporary applications are extremely concrete and specific. He spends a long time arguing that abstinence from alcoholic beverages is not something to be valued in and of itself. John's abstinence was simply a mark by which God separated him out from the mass of peo-ple for a special task.[32] A somewhat amusing example of this kind of spe-cific application is Calvin's application of the texts about the naming of

John (Luke 1:56–64) and Jesus (Luke 2:21). The fact that the names were given with seriousness of purpose should teach us to take the naming of children seriously. Some parents want to give their children "profane names." (Calvin gives as a specific example the name "Claude," whom Calvin refers to derisively as "that marmoset.") Neither are the names of kings suitable for the children of believers—"they are forged in the boutique of Satan," and represent all those who fought furiously against God and his Word.[33]

Throughout the sermons, Calvin emphasizes the universality and contemporaneity of the Gospel message. What is said to Mary, Jesus, Elizabeth, John, Simeon, and other characters of the texts is also said to us.[34] It is easy to see how this line of application could lead Calvin to assert that Christ appears to us, just as he appeared to the first witnesses of the gospel. But now "he is present by the means of the gospel." The gospel is the mirror in which we contemplate his face.[35] This contemplation of Christ is no intellectual exercise in reconstructing history. The Christ who appears in the gospel calls for a response of faith—for a conscious confession of belief.[36] With this background in mind, we can now look more closely at two specific sermons on the birth narratives of the second chapter of Luke.

Calvin begins his sermon on the angel's message to the shepherds by stating a principle that controls all his preaching: "We have already declared that it will not profit us much that the Son of God was born into the world unless we know why he was sent to us and what blessing he has brought to us."[37] The benefit of Christ's incarnation only becomes efficacious when it is appropriated by the believer through faith. The objective, historical events are not enough in themselves; they "will not profit us except we be touched with such a fear and reverence as those shepherds felt."[38]

The angel's message to the shepherds, however, reminds us that our fear of God should be tempered, since he speaks not in judgment but in love and "takes the part of a good and loving Father" who holds his children in his arms.[39] Although we rightly feel dismay at our sins and at the majesty of God's Word, joy abounds when we recognize that God reconciles us to himself in Jesus Christ. This is the joy the angel speaks of—a joy which shall be to all people. And this is especially significant for us, Calvin adds, since we are all Gentiles who were included in God's promise only after the Jews. Here we see Calvin moving the reference of the Gospel story from the past tense to the present. Although the historical facts of the angel's message are, for Calvin, beyond question, the *mere* facts are not enough: they must be appropriated in the believer's own life history.

The Christian's joy in Christ's birth is the same in all times. It cannot be a joy in the pleasures and delights of the world, which "intoxicate" us and draw us away from God. No, it must be like the joy the shepherds experienced after they were away from the manger and returned to their flocks. They did not get any special worldly gain from their knowledge. And neither will our wealth or honor be increased by the gospel. But we can never cease to be caught up in a "spiritual joy," since we have peace with God through Christ. Indeed, our joy must be so great that we can rejoice in our afflictions, knowing that God works through them for good.[40] The joy brought to us by the gospel has its foundation in Jesus Christ, for in Christ God was reconciling the world to himself, "and today he still continues this work when the gospel is preached to us."[41] Note that in the last sentence Calvin equates the reconciling work of Christ in the past with the preaching of the gospel in the present. The work of Christ is not merely an exchange between the Father and the Son in the past, which the believer now appropriates intellectually. Rather, the work of Christ somehow takes place in preaching.

Calvin notes with special care that the angel said the Savior is born to *us*. God planned in advance to answer the doubt of those who say that although the Redeemer is indeed born, it makes no difference for us. The angel proclaims: He is born to you! And if we have Christ, what do we lack in the perfection of wisdom, justice, life, and glory?[42] The angel, Calvin continues, also identified the Savior: he is Christ the Lord, the Anointed One, the receiver of gifts from God's Spirit. Christ received these gifts not for his own use, but so that we might be "participators" in them.[43] We participate when we draw from Christ's fullness, "and it is not necessary for us to make long journeys to come to him, for by the gospel he declares that he is still ours today."[44] Once again, Calvin's overriding concern seems to be the move from the past tense to the present. It is particularly interesting that he denies the need for "long journeys" to come to Christ. The "gospel history" does not imply an unbridgeable gap between the story and the hearer. Rather, Gospel as a genre works in the same way in both the past and the present. The Gospel confronts the hearer with the *presence* of the Son of God.[45]

The reference to Christ's birth in the city of David, Calvin argues, was given as a proof of the authenticity of the angelic message. God had predicted from all eternity that he would send his Son. But though the angel's message should have been enough in itself, God also confirmed it with a great multitude of the heavenly host. He did this because he knew what *we* are like. "That is to say, we are full of wavering . . . and there is nothing but levity and inconstancy in us, and we are bad-tempered . . . [so that] he cannot win us as he should."[46] Since God had to attach such extraordinary confirmations to the gospel, we must take care lest we in our presumption lose our faith. Calvin here even ventures to explain the events narrated within the text with regard to the hearer rather than the immediate context. God sent a multitude of the heavenly host not for the shepherds but for *us*! Through this technique, Calvin draws his hearers into the story and makes it theirs in a more than cognitive way. The hearer does not so much intellectually appropriate the story as *participate* in it.[47]

Calvin has made at least three important moves in this sermon. First, he has insisted that the hearers of a sermon must enter into the Gospel history and participate in the events it records. Second, he has identified preaching as the present locus of the redemptive work of Christ. Third, he has suggested that interpretation of scripture ought to be more concerned with the present than with the past.

In his sermon on the nativity of Jesus, Calvin begins on a striking note: "We know that it is our good, our joy, and rest to be united with the Son of God."[48] That is why we must contemplate Christ's birth, for none of us could have reached so high as to approach him. He had to come to us and make himself our Brother. We must recognize, Calvin tells us, "how our Lord Jesus Christ from his birth so suffered for us that, when we seek him, we need not make long circuits to find him, nor to be truly united to him."[49]

Although for Calvin the historical core of the narratives is taken for granted, the *point* of the "history" of Christ's birth, he tells us, is not to inform us of past events. Rather, in the Gospel history we see "that the Son of God, even our Mediator, has united himself to us in such a way that we must never doubt that we are sharers both of his life and of all his riches," and "we must learn from those who are here ordained as teachers and leaders how we must come to our Lord Jesus Christ."[50] The "teachers" here mentioned are poor shepherds. Not the wise or presumptuous, but the simple of this world show us the way to come to Christ. From them we must learn that the one who would be reputed Christian must be a fool in this world. In particular, we must look at their faith. They were not astonished or repelled by the scandal of the Redeemer's birthplace. They humbly accepted God's Word without questioning what seemed contrary to reason in its presentation.[51] And so it still remains in Christ's church. The Word appears in the words of a mere man, in a "drop of water" in baptism, and in the "piece of bread and drop of wine" of the Eucharist. It seems to us "that such ceremonies which have no great pomp can have no value. So then, we see still better how what is here mentioned about the shepherds pertains to us and how we should profit by it today."[52] Calvin stresses the similarity of Christian experience within the Gospel history and after it. It was no easier for the shepherds to believe that the babe in the manger was the Son of God than it is for us to believe that the words of a mere man can be God's Word. The decision with which faith presents the hearer of the Word is the same in all time, and only two responses to it are possible: belief and unbelief.

Curiously, after this eloquent argument for the wisdom of God, which is a stumbling block to the Jews and folly to the Greeks, Calvin returns to the theme of "proofs" of the Redeemer's identity. "For if the shepherds had had no other sign than the stable and the manger, we could say, 'Look at the poor idiots who make themselves believe foolishly and without reason that he was the Redeemer of the world.' That would be altogether too easy for us. We could, then, be in doubt. But the shepherds were confirmed by other means to be certain that he was the Son of God."[53] They had the testimony of angels and the fulfillment of prophecy. God did not send the angels just for the sake of the shepherds, however, but so that "we might be able to come to our Lord Jesus Christ with a ready courage and that we might no longer be held back by dispute or scruple . . . [from him] by whom God willed to communicate himself to us."[54] The host of angels, the fulfillment of prophecy, all were given more for *us* than for the shepherds, and "that is how we must apply to our use and instruction the things here discussed. For it is not the intention of St. Luke . . . simply to write us a history."[55]

The sermon ends on the same theme with which it began—union with Christ. The message proclaimed by the angels is "that it is now God in us, as much as God with us. Our God with us is declared when he willed to dwell in our human nature as in his temple. But now it is God in us, that is, we feel him joined to us in greater power than when he showed and declared himself mortal man."[56] Calvin seems to be arguing here that, in fact, the believer's communion with Christ is *more*, not less, intimate after his physical departure from the world, and that *we* can know Christ in us as much as, or more than, his earthly companions did. And so it is quite appropriate that the final note of this sermon is a eucharistic one. In the Holy Supper, we may not doubt that "although we perceive only bread and wine . . . [Christ] really dwells in us, and we are so joined to him there is nothing of himself that he is not willing to communicate to us."[57]

In sum, one is struck by the fact that for Calvin the point of the story in Luke 2 lies wholly in what it discloses to us about the presence of Christ today, in our lives. He had no reason to doubt that the narrative was factual, a report of actual events. But would it, one wonders, have totally undermined his message if someone had persuaded him that things very likely did not happen quite the way they are recorded?

## SERMONS ON JESUS' PUBLIC MINISTRY

There are not very many sermons in the collection of the *Calvini opera* that have to do with the period of Jesus' public ministry. For the purpose of illustration, I want to single out two that deal with Jesus' miracle-working activity. The first is on Mark 1:23–27 and Luke 4:33–36, a pericope in which Jesus casts out a demon. It is interesting that Calvin begins the sermon with the statement that "miracles mean nothing unless they are joined with doctrine."[58] Thus it should not be surprising that what follows is a heavily doctrinal sermon. He begins by noting that the demon-possessed man makes a kind of confession about the person of Jesus: he is the Holy One of God. But Calvin is quick to point out that this minimal confession will not suffice for true children of God. For them, it is not enough to know that God is holy and powerful; they must know that God wills to be their Savior in his Son.[59] The knowledge of faith is a particular kind of knowledge of God: its object is God's goodwill toward us. This leads Calvin to a long series of criticisms of the "papists' " understanding of faith, including their notion of formed and unformed faith.[60]

Moving on, Calvin talks about the title that Jesus is given in the demon's confession, "the Holy One of God." This is said in order to single out Jesus Christ the Mediator from the common mass of humans. For even though all children of God can be called "saints," there is an enormous difference between the head and the body. Christ's sanctity is of a different order than any saint's. He alone was born free from the taint of original sin; he alone is altogether perfect; and he alone communicates his perfection for the salvation of others.[61] Nevertheless, the demonic confession is defective because it says nothing of God's goodwill in Jesus.

Not surprisingly, Calvin takes the demon's semblance of piety in confessing the holiness of the Mediator as a point of contact with sixteenth-century experience. The demon is like those today who make a show of revering God the Father, Son, and Spirit, but then insist on adoring Mary, the angels, the saints, and so forth. They are constantly quarreling about merits, acts of supererogation, the way to achieve paradise, and other devotions that bastardize and falsify the service of God.[62] Their confession, therefore, no more represents true piety than does the confession of the demon.

Calvin next turns to the miracle of the exorcism itself. He states: "Let us take in the similarity of this miracle with that which is done in us."[63] For we, too, are, as it were, possessed by the devil until we are delivered by the mercy of Christ. And we cannot possess true faith until we have renounced the devil. The drama of warfare between Christ and the devil goes on inside us as well. Calvin takes the reception of the miracle by the people in the narrative as proof of the purpose of miracles: they are given to confirm the preaching of the gospel. Jesus' word came first, and only then was a work added that demonstrated the power of his word. Once again, Calvin applies the story to his own context by criticizing the practice surrounding miracles in the Roman Church. For the "papists," miracles are not confirmations of the gospel but rather occasions for urging the veneration of saints, prayer to saints, devotion with respect to relics, and other such superstitions on poor people who do not know better. Instead of confirming the gospel, these so-called miracles put the creature before the Creator.[64]

The final section of the sermon returns to doctrine. Calvin points out that the people asked the question, "What new teaching is this?" This question was put in their mouths in order to teach us that, although Christ is the clearest manifestation of the gospel and in that sense new, Christ's teaching cannot be separated from the Law and the Prophets.[65] There is one covenant of grace that spans the Old and New Testaments.

In this sermon we see Calvin focusing more on the doctrine implied by the narrative than on the narrative itself. He never asks the question, "Did this really happen?" The narratives are presumed to refer to factual events. But the historical, literal sense of the texts simply holds no interest for Calvin the preacher. Only as the history is translated into general principles that can be applied to another age—only as it is transmuted from past events to present experience—is the history of interest.

The second sermon I want to single out here is on Matthew 8:14–18, Mark 1:29–39, and Luke 4:38–43. It recounts, among other things, the healing of Peter's mother-in-law. Calvin moves almost immediately to a criticism of Roman exegesis of the passage. The "papists" think that the prayers offered by those around Peter's mother-in-law are proof that saints can be our intercessors and advocates. But this is not so. Rather, the Gospel writers wished to show that in matters of our salvation, we ought each to care for the other and not only look to our own good.[66] Jesus' healing of the fever is taken as an illustration that there are secret movements inside our bodies that we cannot understand; yet we must confess that all these things are in God's control. Thus we do wrong when we murmur about our afflictions. We should, on the contrary, receive them in the confidence that God will take pity on us.[67]

Even though the text speaks of a physical healing, Calvin asserts that this is meant to show what is the fruit of Christ's redemptive passion and death: namely, the healing of our souls. If we focused only on the way in which Christ appeased the wrath of God that we justly deserved, we might be frightened to come to Christ. But the healing miracles of Jesus demonstrate that he is the spiritual medicine for our souls. As he healed paralytics, so he enables us to come to him.[68] Matthew, Calvin argues, really intended to speak of the principle by which we are to understand Christ's work: that there is no health or wholeness in the world that does not proceed from his sheer grace.[69]

The final thing Calvin notes in the text is that Jesus withdrew to pray, and the crowd followed him. This part of the text shows that Jesus was preparing to perform his office as a preacher of the gospel—his prophetic office. Putting oneself in the presence of God is the necessary prerequisite for true prophets.[70] And today Jesus is present in the preaching of the gospel, through those whom he has ordained to be his ministers.[71] Calvin notes that the authority of the Word comes from God and is recognized by the hearers of the Word. That is why the people followed after Jesus. It is also why the authority of ministers today is granted to them by the congregation.[72]

In this sermon as well, Calvin seems to avoid dwelling on the narrative. He is interested in the doctrinal principles that the narrative illustrates, as well as in a contemporary application of them; and he asserts, as is his custom, that Jesus is present today in the preaching of the gospel. But the details of the narrative are simply passed over in silence. Now we must see whether the strategies are the same in his sermons on the death and resurrection of Christ.

## SERMONS ON THE PASSION
## AND RESURRECTION

In his sermon on Matthew 26:67–27:10, Calvin begins by alluding to 1 Corinthians 1:18 and 2 Corinthians 2:15–16, where the gospel is called the odor of life to all whom God calls to salvation and the odor of death to all reprobates who perish. The reading from Matthew 26, Calvin maintains, has to do with two examples that illustrate just this point. Judas, on the one hand, is seized with despair after he betrays Jesus, and so is ultimately condemned. But Peter, whose sin of denial is no less grave, takes this opportunity to receive the gift of salvation. All of this is meant to show us that "unless we are by special grace called to be sharers of the fruit of the death and passion of the Son of God, it will be useless to us. It is not enough . . . that our Lord Jesus Christ has suffered, but the good which he acquired for us must be communicated, and we must come to possess it; and that is done when we are drawn to him in faith."[73]

Peter's denial shows how weak humans are as soon as God has let go of their hands. Even though Peter is exalted as a model disciple, he was unable, when left on his own, to preserve the constancy of his faith in the Redeemer. So believers must constantly ask God to preserve them in faith. Once Peter falters, his situation goes from bad to worse. He is plunged ever more deeply into ruin, and were it not for God's mercy he would perish completely. This too is true of all human beings. It is only through God's forbearance that they are spared from reaching the bottom.[74]

Peter was not left in hopelessness, however. The fact that he went out and wept bitterly after his denial of Christ shows that "already the passion and death of our Lord Jesus Christ was profitable to him," for his tears are a sign of the gift of true repentance.[75] Now Peter's repentance was caused by the glance of the Savior at him as he passed. So, we too will be unable to receive the grace of repentance until Christ has looked upon us. And this is done in the daily preaching of the gospel. But not just in the gospel; the book of nature is also a call for us to return to God.

> Does not all creation incite us to come to God? If our senses are well ruled so as to have some particle of prudence, when the sun rises in the morning, does it not call us to adore our God? After that, if we notice how the earth and all elements perform their offices, the beasts and the trees, that shows us that we must draw up to our God, in order that he may be glorified in us, and that we may not think of doing otherwise. The cock, then, has well crowed, and not only the cock, but God makes all his creatures above and below to crow, to exhort us to come to him.[76]

In short, Christ's call is available not only in the Law and the Prophets and in the preaching of the gospel, but also in the very saturation of nature with evidence of God's wisdom and might.

Calvin takes Judas' pseudorepentance as a symbol of the impossibility of the reconciliation of the reprobate. Judas and the chief priests are stricken with a kind of madness that renders them unable to recognize the folly of their ways. All of this should convince us that, were it not for God's gift of preservation in faith, we should be in just the same position.[77]

Jesus' judgment before Pilate is recorded so that we could be assured that Christ has taken our place before the judgment seat of God. His willingness to stand and be condemned shows that he wills to be our Savior. His silence before his accusers gives us the freedom to call on God with full voice. In short, the events surrounding Jesus' trial before Pilate symbolize the role he plays for us eternally before God the Father.[78]

Calvin begins his sermon on Matthew 27:45–54, after a brief review of the previous day's sermon, with a consideration of some of the historical details of the narrative. Specifically, he is eager to explain the difference between the way time was measured in the biblical world and in his own day. He concludes that Jesus was crucified sometime between 9 A.M. and noon, and that it probably took no more than three hours for him to die.[79] Another detail that particularly interests him is the circumstances that caused darkness to fall during the time of the crucifixion. Was this a general eclipse of the sun? Calvin thinks not, for this would obscure the miracle that God wanted to show. Rather, the sun's disappearance was a true miracle that God wrought to symbolize how all the creatures on earth ought to hide from the horror of what was happening to Jesus. Moreover, the sun itself was showing its homage to Christ by hiding its face.[80] Finally, Calvin also notes that, when Jesus cries out "My God, my God, why have you forsaken me?" it is given in Syriac (Aramaic)—and not in the same spelling by all the evangelists. That is because when the Jews returned from Babylon their language was never pure Syriac again. But this historical detail has *theological* significance: Calvin thinks "God willed especially that this be recited in two tongues, to show that it was something important."[81]

After these historical reflections, Calvin moves the text toward doctrinal issues. Jesus' cry of dereliction shows that his perfect obedience to the Father rendered satisfaction for all our sins. Although scripture often says we are redeemed by the blood of Christ, this is said in accommodation to human weakness. We are reminded thereby of the visible, physical event of Jesus' death. But, Calvin maintains, "the death and passion of our Lord Jesus would not have served anything to wipe away the iniquities of the world except insofar as he obeyed, indeed, abasing himself to so frightful a death."[82] In our place, Christ suffered the horror of absolute alienation from God.

The next theological matter taken up is how the two natures in Christ, divine and human, intended the cry of dereliction. In his divine nature, surely, Christ could have had no doubts. But even in his human nature, Calvin argues, he had perfect faith in God that was never shaken. The very cry of dereliction demonstrates this, because Jesus addressed his question to the Father, in whom he trusted. "He sought confirmation of his faith so that he might always persist in invoking God."[83] Indeed, "in our Lord Jesus there was nothing troubled or disordered. . . . He was not so seized with anguish, that he did not have his hope fixed rightly on God."[84]

The mockery of those around the cross is a point of contact with sixteenth-century experience. The papists mock the preaching of the Reformers and challenge its fruitfulness. But this is true not only of the Roman priests but also of "belligerent people among us" who blaspheme the gospel. Since Satan today spends so much energy sharpening the tongues of his agents to "spit his venom" against the purity of doctrine, it should not seem strange to us that Jesus also suffered these rebukes.[85]

Jesus' last words are an assurance of the sufficiency of his sacrifice for the sins of the world. He was offered as a sacrifice once, to sanctify us perpetually. Thus the Roman Church and its priests usurp Jesus' own office of priest by claiming to offer a daily sacrifice in the Mass.[86] Calvin concludes this sermon by speaking of how the benefits of Christ's passion and death are immediately available to those whom he draws to him by his gospel. The drama of death and resurrection is, in a sense, repeated in every Christian's experience: "For when we shall be cast down to the very bottom of the abyss of death, it is Christ's office to withdraw us from it and to lead us to the heavenly inheritance which he has so dearly acquired for us."[87]

The sermon on Matthew 27:55–60, on the burial of the body of Jesus, is also mainly a series of doctrinal reflections. Calvin first notes that the women were those who remained around Jesus' cross until the end. The fact that this is emphasized by the Gospel writer is in order that we may learn that God perfects his power in weakness. The women's following of Jesus showed their inclination to receive the fruit of the gospel. Even when it appeared that Jesus' cause was lost, the women remained around him in faith, waiting in the expectation that his promises to them would be fulfilled. So we must learn to rely on Christ even when what he has promised does not at first glance seem to have been fulfilled.[88] Joseph and Nicodemus are examples similar to the women. Neither of them had been bold disciples of Jesus during his public ministry, but now they step in to do what even the twelve disciples dared not. And they, too, waited in expectation of the coming of Christ's kingdom. The Holy Spirit put these examples in scripture so that we could learn, "when everything will be confused and in despair, to have our eyes fixed upon God."[89]

Calvin next considers a matter that is not even given in the narrative of the text for his sermon: namely, John's statement that before Jesus was taken down from the cross, the soldiers pierced his side, and water and blood flowed out. After a brief dalliance with a scientific explanation of this matter ("It is true that the blood congeals in death . . . and that with the blood water can come . . . since the color and the thickest part of the blood will have coagulated"), Calvin offers two explanations of it.[90] First, the piercing is meant to show that Jesus is our purity and that we must look to him to cleanse us from the stain of sin. And, second, the blood and water represent the sacraments of Baptism and the Lord's Supper, by which we receive a sign and seal of what Jesus accomplished for us in his death.[91]

The final matter that Calvin takes up in this sermon is the burial of Jesus. He turns first to the question of burial practice: Was it not wrong for Jesus to allow these lavish preparations of his body for the grave if he really wished to show forth the promise of his resurrection? The answer is offered by means of a historical explanation. The Jewish custom of the day included these practices—all of them pointing forward to the hope of resurrection. Jesus allowed this manner of burial to be performed on him because he had not yet fulfilled the final act of resurrection. But now Christians ought to favor simple burials in expectation of the resurrection that has been manifested already in Jesus Christ.[92]

The burial of Jesus, however, also teaches a profound theological lesson: that if we wish to rise with Christ, we must also be buried with him into death. Calvin states:

We must die not only once, but we must suffer patiently to be buried until the end. I call it death when God wills that we endure so for his name. For though we are not at first dragged to the fire or condemned by the world, yet, when we are afflicted there is already a species of death which we must endure patiently. . . . For as the devil never ceases to plan what is possible for him to distract and debauch us, so all our lifetime we must not cease to fight against him. Although this condition may be hard and tedious, let us wait for the time to come when God calls us to himself.[93]

The burial of Jesus is an incitement to perseverance in faith and hope for the future.

The final sermon I wish to discuss briefly in this section is on the resurrection (Matt. 28:1–10).[94] It is the only sermon on this subject that survives in the *Calvini opera*. Calvin begins the sermon with the scandalous fact that women were the first witnesses of the resurrection. Why was this the case? For one thing, God wished to punish the disciples for their temerity, and so he humiliated them in having to receive his Word from the mouths of women. This leads to the general theological principle that all of us are obliged to accept God's Word as it comes to us, even when preached by weak and imperfect human vessels.[95]

This sermon is somewhat different from the three previous sermons on the passion of Jesus. Calvin is less inclined to speak at length about particular doctrines; rather, he jumps back and forth from a simple retelling of the story to a baldly stated interpretation of the meaning of each person and event for us. In rapid succession he discusses the nature of true faith, the value of works, the terror that the wicked must feel at the manifestation of God's power, and the accommodation by which Christ makes himself available to us even in our weakness.[96]

The other distinctive feature of this sermon is that Calvin repeats over and over an invitation for his hearers to come to Christ.[97] Jesus wills us to come to him, "and he does not wait for us to look for him, but he has provided that we might be called by the preaching of the Gospel and that this message might be spoken by the mouths of his heralds."[98] This emphasis on the calling of Christ and the hearers' movement toward him may be explained by the fact that this sermon was preached before the celebration of Communion on Easter Day. These are "comfortable words" of invitation, intended to reassure the congregation that the gift of the Table is for them. It is appropriate, then, that Calvin ends with the theme of union with Christ:

Let us realize the unity that we have with our Lord Jesus Christ, that is, he is willing to have a common life with us, and that what he has may be ours, even that he wishes to dwell in us, not in imagination, but in fact; . . . that he so works by the power of his Holy Spirit that we are united to him more than are the members of a body.[99]

The whole sermon, then, may be seen as an invitation to the Table that is issued by Christ himself—the present Christ, who speaks through the mouth of his minister.[100]

## CALVIN'S SERMONS ON THE GOSPELS
## AND NARRATIVE INTERPRETATION

We have discovered that Calvin rarely takes an interest in the historical grounding of the biblical texts. When he does, the things that fascinate him seem to be the least significant: for example, not *that* Jesus was born from a virgin mother, but *why* Matthew chose that word to render the text from Isaiah; not *that* Jesus really died and was buried, but *why* the particular burial practice recounted in the narrative was the one that was used. This illustrates amply, it seems, that Calvin simply assumes the historicity of the texts. He takes it for granted that the narrated events really happened in a very similar fashion to what the text records.

But we have also discovered that Calvin is rarely satisfied to confine himself to the actual words of the narratives or to the narrated events when he is preaching. He moves constantly from text to meaning, from words to doctrine, and from doctrine to the contemporary problems of being a Christian in sixteenth-century Geneva. Moreover, Calvin uses these strategies of interpretation not only on poetic texts, or in interpreting discourses of Jesus, but also in understanding the supposedly historical events themselves. The events and characters of the narratives mean something *more* than what they may seem to on the face of it. The narratives tell us not only about the world of the past, but also about general principles of Christian theology, and about the nature of Christian experience.

One could argue that there is nothing particularly original about this way of interpreting the Gospel narratives. The fourfold exegesis of the Middle Ages—literal, allegorical, tropological, anagogical—in its own way did much the same thing. And although the Reformers of the sixteenth century supposedly rejected this model of interpretation in favor of a more strictly literal or historical reading of the text, it is not altogether clear (at least from a reading of Calvin's sermons) that they achieved their aspirations. Calvin is certainly critical of what he takes to be capricious allegorical interpretation (such as the number mysticism of which his hero Augustine was so fond). But when he asserts that a reference to the darkening of the sun at the hour of Jesus' death shows that Jesus is the Sun of Righteousness, he is not so very far from allegory; and his contemporary applications of texts are not unlike the tropological interpretations of his medieval forebears.

One distinctive feature of Calvin's interpretation of the Gospel texts, however, is his emphasis on the presence of Christ in the proclamation. The Gospel not only tells us about Jesus in the past, but also, and more importantly, is the manifestation of Christ in the present. We do not need to make long journeys to find him and be united to him, for he speaks to us just as truly as he spoke to the first disciples. As we have seen, Calvin sometimes even goes so far as to assert that somehow *we* have a richer experience of the presence of Christ than did the eyewitnesses to his life. Thus, although Calvin does not question the truth of the history recounted in the Gospels, it is almost entirely irrelevant to him, both for interpretative and for theological reasons, to assert its truth.

It is difficult for me to see, then, how Calvin can be the purest example of precritical "narrative" exegesis, as Hans Frei asserts. If we remind ourselves of the three presuppositions of the precritical hermeneutic that Frei lays out, it is really only the first that applies without qualification to Calvin. That is, Calvin did assume that the biblical story "referred to and described actual historical occurrences." In his sermons, the historicity of narrated events is never a question for Calvin.[101] What is interesting is that the history, the sequence of events, seems to be of no particular interest to him either.

Frei's second precritical hermeneutical assumption—"that the various biblical stories described a single real world of one temporal sequence" which can be united into one story—cannot apply to Calvin's preaching without qualifications.[102] On the one hand, Calvin does affirm one covenant of grace that spans the two testaments of the Bible. All the stories are attempts to trace God's gracious dealings with the elect. But in his sermons Calvin is not interested in tying together the individual narratives of the Synoptic Gospels as one continuous story—not even to compose a coherent biography of Jesus. Rather, the individual narratives are taken as individually representing a coherent picture of the nature of Christian faith.

Finally, the precritical presupposition that "the world truly rendered by combining the biblical narratives . . . must in principle embrace the experience of any present age and reader" can also be accepted only in a qualified sense.[103] It is true that Calvin believed the texts would have something to say to his sixteenth-century congregation. But this seems nothing more than the formal requirement for interpreting any classic text—the thing that makes it worth reading again. What he does not so clearly presuppose, at least in his preaching, is that the manner of relating the text and present experience is easy and straightforward. The texts need to be translated from one time and culture to another, and sometimes Calvin admits that details of the narrative are simply incapable of being transferred to another time and place.

The sermons on the Synoptic Gospels reveal a Calvin unlike the one Frei discovers in the *Institutes* and the commentaries on Genesis and Isaiah: he is an interpreter who thinks the task is much more than comprehending the meaning of the cumulative sequence of the narrative.[104] In fact, the narrative sequence almost never matters for Calvin in these sermons. One might say of his sermons on the Synoptics what Frei said of Schleiermacher's exegesis: that the narratives refer to something else and so mean something different from what they strictly say.[105]

We must now turn to a closer examination of Schleiermacher's theology of preaching and his sermons on the Gospel narratives. Only then will we be in a position to judge whether he is developing the tradition he received from Calvin, or departing from it in part or in whole.

## NOTES

1. Erwin Mülhaupt, *Die Predigt Calvins: ihre Geschichte, ihre Form, und ihre Religiöse Grundgedanken*, Arbeiten zur Kirchengeschichte, vol. 18 (Berlin and Leipzig: Walter de Gruyter, 1931), 15–16.

2. Dieter Schellong, *Calvins Auslegung der synoptischen Evangelien*, Forschungen zur Geschichte und Lehre des Protestantismus, vol. 38 (Munich: Chr. Kaiser Verlag, 1969), 24–34.

3. *CO* 46:iii–iv. Calvin preached a series of sermons on the history of the passion and resurrection on at least three occasions—in 1549, 1550, and 1553—always starting on the Sunday before Easter and culminating on Easter Day (T.H.L. Parker, *Calvin's Preaching* [Louisville, Ky.: Westminster/John Knox Press, 1992], 160–62). Many of the volumes of Calvin's sermons that were included in the earliest catalogs of his works were sold to a bookseller simply for the value of the paper on which they were written, and subsequently lost. See T.H.L. Parker, *The Oracles of God*, 163–65.

4. *OS* I:82. Presumably, Calvin means that the birth and death themselves have a significance for salvation that the rest of Jesus' life does not. However, in *Inst.* 2.16.5, he is careful to argue that Christ abolished sin and acquired righteousness not only in death but by "the whole course of his obedience."

5. T.H.L. Parker, *Calvin's Preaching*, 79–92, 131–38. Cf. T.H.L. Parker, *The Oracles of God*, 65–80.

6. *CO* 46:90, 231.

7. *CO* 46:226–32, 246.

8. *CO* 46:325–26, 350.

9. *CO* 46:63.

10. *CO* 46:65.

11. *CO* 46:73.

12. *CO* 46:114, 118, 126, 143.

13. When I use the word "symbol" in the following discussion, I mean by it nothing more than the common dictionary sense of the term, "that which stands for something else."

14. *CO* 46:275, 278.

15. *CO* 46:280.

16. *CO* 46:308–9.

17. *CO* 46:326.

18. *CO* 46:34.

19. *CO* 46:51.

20. *CO* 46:70.

21. *CO* 46:340–41.

22. *CO* 46:75.

23. *CO* 46:122.

24. *CO* 46:64–65.

25. *CO* 46:151, 269, 357–58, 309, 404, 417, 420, 423–24. The Seven Dolors of Mary are counted in different ways, but all lists include the crucifixion and burial of Jesus. The Stabat Mater is a hymn written specifically for this feast day. The feast of the Joys of Mary is suggested by the "joyful mysteries" of the rosary. See the article on "Marian Feasts," in *New Catholic Encyclopedia*, vol. 9 (New York: McGraw-Hill Book Co., 1967), 210–12; cf. the article on "Mary, Mother of Jesus Christ," in *The New Schaff-Herzog Encyclopedia of Religious Knowledge*, ed. Samuel Macauley Jackson et al., 12 vols. (New York and London: Funk & Wagnalls, 1908–14), 7:219–24.

26. *CO* 46:97.

27. *CO* 46:412.

28. *CO* 46:32. Rituals surrounding the feast of St. John the Baptist, including the lighting of fires to ward away evil spirits, were some of the last remnants of pagan culture to pervade Europe, even after the introduction of Protestantism. See Jean Delumeau, *Catholicism between Luther and Voltaire: A New View of the Counter-Reformation,* trans. Jeremy Moiser (London: Burns & Oates, 1977), 167, 177–79.

29. *CO* 46:251.

30. *CO* 46:300–301.

31. *CO* 46:341–42.

32. *CO* 46:35–36.

33. *CO* 46:154–55, 321. Actually, the naming of children presented for baptism was the source of a serious conflict between Calvin and some of the citizens of Geneva. "Claude" was a particularly reprehensible name for Calvin because there had been a statue of St. Claude in the town, and people believed that naming their children after the saint would bring them good fortune. Calvin asked the town council to pass an ordinance forbidding the use of certain names and this became law on November 22, 1546. A list of approved names was provided. See R. N. Carew Hunt, *Calvin* (London: Centenary Press, 1933), 168.

34. *CO* 46:63, 82, 103, 378.

35. *CO* 46:283, 378.

36. On this point Max Dominicé has put it nicely: "For Calvin, to speak of Jesus Christ never means to speak of a religious personality from the past over against whom we relate as observers with the task of judging him or her, of understanding and explaining his character traits, his discourses and his actions. . . . To speak of Jesus Christ means, for Calvin, precisely not to speak of him as a spectator, but as a believer and witness who is totally engaged in what he says, who confesses Jesus, who proclaims Christ" ("Die Christusverkündigung bei Calvin," in *Jesus Christus im Zeugnis der heiligen Schrift und der Kirche,* eine Vortragsreihe von Dr. R. L. Schmidt, Dr. E. Gaugler, Dr. R. Bultmann, Dr. U. Gelg, Dr. E. Wolf, M. Dominicé, 2d ed. [Munich: Chr. Kaiser Verlag, 1936], 223–53; quote is on 227–28). For a somewhat different perspective on the importance of the historical in Calvin's preaching, see Denis Müller, "L'Element historique dans la prédication de Calvin: un aspect original de l'homilétique du Réformateur," *Revue d'histoire et*

*de philosophie religieuses* 64 (1984): 365–86, esp. 378–82. Cf. Dieter Schellong, *Calvins Auslegung der synoptischen Evangelien*, 160–64.

37. *Serm. Luke 2:9–14 (CO* 46:285).

38. *CO* 46:286.

39. Ibid.

40. *CO* 46:289–90.

41. *CO* 46:291.

42. *CO* 46:292.

43. This closely parallels Calvin's discussion of the three offices of Christ in the *Institutes,* where Christ is said to have received the gifts peculiar to each office not only for himself, but also to share with believers in the church (*Inst.,* 2.15 [ET, 1:494–503]).

44. *CO* 46:293.

45. *Comm. Harmony of the Gospels (CO* 45:1). The second epigraph to this chapter aptly expresses Calvin's understanding of this (*Comm. John* 7:33 [*CO* 47:178]).

46. *CO* 46:295.

47. This is not, however, what I take Hans Frei to mean when he speaks about narrative interpretation embracing the experience of any age or reader. Frei sees the connection between the text and the reader's experience largely in terms of the one history-like narrative that connects them. In other words, the story that began "back there" in the biblical narratives continues with my story in the present. When Calvin draws his hearers into the text, he does so by speaking in general categories about what the experience of faith is like and in asserting a homogeneity between the experience of faith in the past and in the present.

48. *Serm. Luke 2:1–14 (CO* 46:955).

49. *CO* 46:956.

50. *CO* 46:958.

51. *CO* 46:958–59.

52. *CO* 46:960.

53. *CO* 46:961.

54. *CO* 46:964.

55. *CO* 46:963.

56. *CO* 46:966.

57. *CO* 46:966. See Fritz Büsser, "Weihnachtspredigten Lk. 2, 1–14," in *Théorie et pratique de l'exégèse: Actes du troisième colloque international sur l'histoire de l'exégèse biblique du XVIe siècle,* ed. Irena Backus and Francis Higman (Geneva: Droz, 1990), 127–40, esp. 135–36.

58. *CO* 46:734.

59. *CO* 46:736.

60. *CO* 46:737–38; cf. *Inst.,* 3.11.8–10 (ET, 1:734–38).

61. *CO* 46:739–40.

62. *CO* 46:743.

63. *CO* 46:744.

64. *CO* 46:745–46.

65. *CO* 46:746–47.

66. *CO* 46:750–51.

67. *CO* 46:751–52.

68. *CO* 46:753–54.

69. *CO* 46:755.

70. *CO* 46:756.

71. *CO* 46:757.

72. *CO* 46:758–59.

73. *CO* 46:874–75.

74. *CO* 46:876.

75. *CO* 46:878–79.

76. *CO* 46:879–80.

77. *CO* 46:883.

78. *CO* 46:886–88.

79. *CO* 46:916–17.

80. *CO* 46:917–18.

81. *CO* 46:918.

82. *CO* 46:920.

83. *CO* 46:921–22.

84. *CO* 46:922. This is very similar to the interpretation of the cry of dereliction that Schleiermacher gives. See p. 88 below. It is particularly this aspect of Schleiermacher's understanding of Jesus that offends Karl Barth (*Die Theologie Schleiermachers*, 155–57) and Hans Frei (*The Eclipse of the Biblical Narrative*, 313–24). But Barth's harshest criticisms could apply equally well to Calvin's account of the death of Jesus.

85. *CO* 46:923.

86. *CO* 46:924–25.

87. *CO* 46:928.

88. *CO* 46:929–31.

89. *CO* 46:931–33.

90. *CO* 46:934.

91. *CO* 46:935–36.

92. *CO* 46:936–38. Interestingly, Calvin here does something he rarely does in the sermons I have studied: he compares the biblical history to general world history in noting that the Egyptians had even more elaborate burial rituals. But since they used these ceremonies as preparation for great mourning, it is clear that the devil had bewitched them into perverting the proper order of things (*CO* 46:937).

93. *CO* 46:940.

94. For a discussion of the rhetorical devices used in this sermon, see Olivier Millet, "Sermon sur la Résurrection: quelques remarques sur l'homilétique de Calvin," *Bulletin de la Société de l'Histoire du Protestantisme Français* 134 (1988): 683–92.

95. *CO* 46:943–44.

96. *CO* 46:947–50.

97. *CO* 46:947, 949, 951, 952–53. See Olivier Millet, "Sermon sur la Résurrection," 685–86.

98. *CO* 46:951.

99. *CO* 46:953.

100. See Olivier Millet, "Sermon sur la Résurrection," 685.

101. See Frei, *The Eclipse of the Biblical Narrative*, 2–3. If I may be permitted a digression here, the question of whether Calvin presupposed the historicity of the texts becomes more difficult when one looks at his commentaries. There Calvin is not beyond pointing to "errors" in the text that might suggest the author's account

of the events was not accurate. However, Calvin never went as far as Origen in suggesting that some texts had *no* literal meaning—i.e., no reference to actual historical events. For more on Calvin's attitude toward the biblical narratives, see John T. McNeill, "The Significance of the Word of God for Calvin," *Church History* 28 (1959): 131–46, esp. 137–45.

102. Frei, *The Eclipse of the Biblical Narrative*, 2–3.
103. Ibid.
104. Ibid., 18–37.
105. Ibid., 300–324.

# 4

# SCHLEIERMACHER
# ON THE WORD MADE FLESH

The verse John 1:14 is the basic text for all dogmatics, just as it should be for the conduct of the ministry as a whole.

*On the Glaubenslehre*

If we conceive the incarnation of Christ as the beginning of the regeneration of the whole human race, then the erection of a permanent place for the preaching of the Gospel amongst a people is the beginning of that people's regeneration.

*The Christian Faith*

Schleiermacher's preference for the Gospel of John has often been noted, not least by Schleiermacher himself, who tried, in his lectures on the life of Jesus, to argue for the Fourth Gospel's priority to the Synoptics.[1] The words and images of John's Gospel, and especially those of its prologue, saturate Schleiermacher's theological writing and sermons. In the present chapter it will be our task to show how thoroughly Schleiermacher incorporated the Johannine message into his concept of preaching. For it is the incarnation of the divine *Logos* that serves as Schleiermacher's primary metaphor for the act of preaching.[2] This incarnational view is closely related to Calvin's concept of the sacramental Word, and, like Calvin's, his view of preaching entails a particular disposition toward the biblical texts that permits him to be relatively indifferent to questions about their historicity. Before turning explicitly to Schleiermacher's theology of preaching, however, it will be necessary to consider his theory of religious language and his technical recommendations for the construction of sermons, for they provide the theoretical grounding for his theology of preaching.

## PREACHING AND THE THEORY
## OF RELIGIOUS LANGUAGE

To provide a theory of religious language, according to Schleiermacher's *Brief Outline on the Study of Theology*, is a task for practical theology,[3] and it is in his posthumously published lectures on *Practical Theology* (1850) that he develops his own theory of religious language most thoroughly. But already in earlier works we can discover important elements of Schleiermacher's view of religious speech. One could argue, for example, that communication theory is central to Schleiermacher's argument in the first edition of the *Speeches on Religion* (1799). It operates in at least two ways. First, in describing the problem of the cultured despisers' alienation from religion, Schleiermacher asserts that they have not heard the true "ambassadors from God" and "mediators between limited man and infinite humanity." Rather, they have mistaken the constricted preaching of the state church for true religious communication.[4] Thus, instead of being led by communication to the depths of true religion, the cultured despisers have been misinformed and misdirected. The problem is a *communication* problem. Authentic religious language mediates between humanity and the Infinite. The cultured despisers, therefore, need only identify the true preachers of religion (in the *Speeches* they are more likely to be poets, musicians, or scientists than clergy) and they will perhaps find themselves "infected" with it.[5]

The second way in which communication theory operates in the *Speeches* is in elaborating the very definition of religion that Schleiermacher seeks to develop there. For religion as "sense and taste for the Infinite" does not exist in the isolation of individual religious heroes' internal intuition, but only in community. "Once there is religion," Schleiermacher notes, "it must necessarily also be social. That not only lies in human nature but also is preeminently in the nature of religion."[6] And it is the communication of religion that creates religious communities. The desire for mutual communication, to be both a speaker and a hearer, drives religious people together. Moreover, it is unthinkable that one "retain within himself that [religious feeling] which most strongly forces him out of himself and which, like nothing else, impresses him with the fact that he cannot know himself in and of himself alone."[7] Even if human beings were not social creatures, religion itself is necessarily communicative. And so Schleiermacher elaborates a rather complex communication theory as a part of his understanding of the nature of religion.

As one might expect from what has already been said, religious language has a twofold function: it is used for the cultivation and expansion of true religion (its social function) and as a tool for expressing the encounter between the individual and the Infinite (its representational function). Schleiermacher distinguishes in the fourth speech between the true and invisible church of all religious people and the existing church. The latter always contains many who are not truly religious. Thus, the social purpose of religious language is to gather the true church through the power of mutual communication and to bring more and more people into it. There is no question, however, of forcing one form of religious expression on others. "Nothing at all is said here about the endeavor to make others like ourselves, or about the belief in the indispensability for everyone of what is in us," Schleiermacher states.[8] Even if such proselytization were a desirable thing, it would be impossible, since human beings are active even in the receptive state of listening and can hear only what they are prepared to hear.[9] Religious communication would remain essential, however, even if all human beings were members of the true church, for in the religious experience itself there is a drive or compulsion to expression.[10] Those who, in religious ecstasy, encounter the Infinite, "must [afterward] set down in pictures or words the impression it made on them as an object so as to enjoy it themselves afresh," and they must also "represent for others what they have encountered."[11] One of Schleiermacher's favorite metaphors for this second, representational function of religious language is that of light reflecting individual objects and so producing a variety of colors. The ever-repeated separation of light rays into the spectrum and their reunion in pure light is like the encounter of individuals with the Infinite: always the same in itself, the Infinite appears differently when reflected through different subjects. Even when all humans have been brought into the true church, such religious communication will continue.[12]

> Individuals would then silently light the way for themselves and for others, and the communication of holy thoughts and feelings would consist only in the easy game of now unifying the different beams of this light and then again breaking them up, now scattering it and then again concentrating here and there on individual objects.[13]

The vision of perfection, then, calls not for an end of religious communication, but for greater mutuality, so that all persons can be both stimulative and receptive in communication—in short, so that no individuals are any longer privileged ambassadors of God.[14] In the true church, order is charismatically derived, and each takes turn presenting himself to others for their enrichment, as well as listening to others.[15]

In summary, the *Speeches* present a view of religious language as rhetorical, representational, and mutual or reciprocal. It is rhetorical in the sense that its purpose is to persuade or move those who hear it, and the organization of parts within the whole aims to achieve that end.[16] Religious language is representational in the sense that it embodies or graphically depicts events of experience in order to make them present again. The encounter between the finite and the Infinite that grounds religious language is, therefore, made present again each time the language is spoken.[17] And this feature of religious language contributes in no small part to its rhetorical power. Finally, religious language is mutual or reciprocal in that no one finite being can fully represent the Infinite. And since the purpose of religious language is to mediate between finitude and the Infinite, that mediation will be complete only when every finite being has reflected Infinity in its own mode.[18]

Schleiermacher's discussion of communication theory in the *Speeches*, however, does little to distinguish between the varieties of religious speech. As early as 1797, he had begun to think about the difference genre made for religious language.[19] Poetic, rhetorical, or logical organization of language issues in very different results, and the final products will be suitable only in specific situations. The distinctions between varieties of religious speech are worked out explicitly only in the second edition of *The Christian Faith* (1830–31), although one can detect some of the substance of these distinctions in earlier works as well.[20] Schleiermacher arrives at these distinctions in his discussion of the relation of dogmatics to Christian piety in the introduction ( §§ 15–19). His purpose is to define the specific characteristics of dogmatic or theological language and to distinguish it from other types of religious communication.

The discussion begins with Schleiermacher's account of the emergence of religious language. Religious emotions (*Erregungen*) have in common with other modifications of affective self-consciousness that as soon as they have achieved a certain level or determinateness they present themselves outwardly through facial features and movements of voice and gesture. But in order for a person's religious emotions to become an object of his or her own reflection, they must be renderable in speech. Schleiermacher admits that thinking, even internally, cannot proceed without speech. Language of some sort accompanies all experience. But the specific language that makes up the propositions of Christian faith has reached a degree of specificity that allows for its communicability. "The entire effectiveness of the Redeemer himself was conditioned by the communicability of his self-consciousness by means of speech, and Christianity has, in the same way, always and everywhere spread through proclamation alone."[21] As in the *Speeches*, language here seems to have both a social and a representational function. But unlike his earlier discussion, Schleiermacher goes on in § 15 to describe three kinds of religious language that emerged in Christian proclamation: poetic, rhetorical, and descriptively didactic (*darstellend belehrende*).

It is primarily the last type—the descriptively didactic—that preoccupies Schleiermacher in this context, since it is properly the language of dogmatic propositions, but he does say a good deal about the other two types of language as well. Each type is characterized by both its source and its goal. Poetic expression issues from within in a moment of inspiration and its goal is to represent (*darstellen*) or picture (*bilden*) the inner experience in the broadest possible terms for others.[22] Rhetorical language arises when one is urged from outside the self to communicate in defense or commendation of religious experience or to promote and discipline religious feeling, and its goal is to move (*bewegen*) another.[23] The third type of language, Schleiermacher states, arises when poetic and rhetorical language need to be understood and appropriated by hearers, and its goal is to teach and to transmit what is contained in the other two forms of language. Schleiermacher identifies this third type as the language of confession, and alternately as didactic or descriptive instructional language. The goal of teaching and appropriating religious language demands a kind of clarity or precision, and so didactic language is disciplined by the scientific spirit.[24] But because it is meant to be descriptive of the other two types of religious language, logical or dialectical interest can be understood only as applying to the form and not the content of didactic expression.[25]

The further specification of the varieties of religious language moves beyond the implicit communication theory of the *Speeches* in several ways. First, it has distinguished two varieties of religious language that are somewhat conflated in the *Speeches:* the poetic and the rhetorical. Schleiermacher tends to argue there that all religious language emerges from within (poetic) but that most or all religious language is also driven by the need to move another (rhetorical). By the second edition of the *Glaubenslehre* he takes these to be distinct but not unrelated forms of communication. Second, he develops with much greater clarity a third type of religious language, the didactic, that appears only briefly in the *Speeches*. Third, he connects his theory of religious language explicitly with the proclamation of Christ. To this we shall need to return in due course.

In the introduction to the *Glaubenslehre*, then, Schleiermacher further develops a general theory of religious language that had occupied him for thirty-odd years. We must now consider what this theory meant specifically for the construction of sermons in the Christian church, and so we turn to the *Practical Theology*.

## THE THEORY OF RELIGIOUS SPEECH
## IN THE PRACTICAL THEOLOGY

Already in his *Brief Outline on the Study of Theology* (1811), Schleiermacher argued that the form of religious speech that prevails in Protestant worship—the sermon—is simply an accidental or chance (*zufällig*) development, connected with the peculiar history of the Reformation churches. There could be other forms of valid religious speech, and these also need to be taken into account. But, unfortunately, the discipline of homiletics presupposes that the sermon is the established form of religious speech and thus derives all its rules from it. "It would be better," Schleiermacher argues, "to let go of this restriction and to treat the subject in a more general and freer fashion."[26] It is not surprising, then, that when he developed the outline for his *Practical Theology* in lectures, he dealt with "homiletics" in a rather unconventional way.[27]

The *Practical Theology* is divided into two main parts: the first deals with church service (*Kirchendienst*) and the second with church government (*Kirchenregiment*). The theory of religious speech falls in the first main section, in a discussion of the organization of worship (*Cultus*). Each of the elements of worship—hymns, prayers, sermons, sacraments—as well as its organization has a corresponding theory. So Schleiermacher discusses in turn the theories of liturgy, music, prayer, and religious speech. He purposefully avoids speaking of this last section as a "homiletics," and uses the term "religious speech" (*religiöse Rede*) rather than "sermon" or "preaching" (*Predigt*) to refer to the subject matter of the theory. Schleiermacher expounds the theory of religious speech in much greater length and complexity than any of the other theories, but that is appropriate because speech is the general means of representation in worship.[28] His theory of religious speech begins with an introduction, and then discusses four themes: the coherence (*Einheit*) of religious speech, its arrangement, the invention or production of the thoughts that make up religious speech, and its expression. For Schleiermacher, religious speech is more a question of art (*Kunst*) than of science (*Wissenschaft*), and the organization of his theory is designed to account for the emergence of an actual artifact of religious speech.[29]

The introduction is a rather rambling discussion of the nature and limits of religious speech. The speaker[30] comes forward both as an organ of the community and as one presenting something genuinely his own. The form of religious speech is accidental, so in order to understand it we have to go back to the concept itself: it is a connected series of thoughts whose purpose is to enliven the religious consciousness, to edify the hearer. Certain limits for religious speech are suggested even by this rather abstract definition.[31]

The first set of limits have to do with the speaker and his relationship to the congregation and the denomination. He must not say things that would constitute breaks with the unity of his denomination, but at the same time he must take his point of departure from the actual situation of his congregation. And it is important that the speaker represent the totality of his religious experience to his hearers. That is to say, religious speech must be thoroughly *personal*, incarnate in the person of the speaker. Finally, the speaker should set the length of his discourse based on the congregation's ability to follow. In some places, such as Holland, people are accustomed to listening to long sermons, while elsewhere it would be better to be brief.[32]

The second set of limits have to do with the character of religious speech itself. It must, of course, be *religious* speech, in Schleiermacher's own special definition of religion as feeling (*Anschauung* and *Gefühl*). To speak in another mode, for example about the advantages or usefulness of something, is to transgress the boundaries of the pulpit. Similarly, to introduce technical, theoretical terms, such as those that explain the doctrine of the Trinity, into religious speech is not appropriate. Polemics and politics are special cases, for in each the speaker must weigh his duty to engage the congregation's experience against his obligation to enliven their religious consciousness. Some polemics, for example against irreligion, may be necessary, but an entire sermon devoted to an attack on another group is certainly too much. And there may be cases in which a congregation is so moved by political events, for example in times of war, that to overlook them would be a fault on the speaker's part. Nevertheless, the main goal of religious speech must always be to move or edify the hearer.[33]

### The Coherence of Religious Speech

The coherence of religious speech is necessary for its effectiveness. Schleiermacher discusses it in two ways: objectively, with regard to the *content* of the speech, and subjectively, with regard to the task of producing and receiving such speech. In the evangelical church, religious speech expresses its coherence through text and topic. They are like two foci of an ellipse, and any dissolution of their bond represents a failure in coherence. If it can be said that a speech (sermon) on a particular text totally missed the point of the text when determining its topic, coherence is destroyed. Likewise, if it can be said of a speech on a particular topic that one text would be just as good as the next in addressing it, that is a mistake. The form of religious speech called "homily" receives its coherence from the text alone, but it too has a proper place in evangelical worship.[34]

At this point Schleiermacher interjects a section on the selection and use of texts. "In using the texts, there is an assimilation between the passages of scripture and the speaker: both the tone and the strength of his religious consciousness is a reconstruction of these in the author of the text, and thus it is natural that the text represents more the subjective than the objective side of coherence."[35] That is, the speaker must come to have the same religious consciousness that the author of the biblical text had through an act of empathic imagination. At the same time, the biblical texts themselves present the objective coherence of ordered content in that their authors were also reconstructing the religious experience of the person or communities about whom they wrote. The most correct use of scripture, then, is one in which the inner disposition (*Gemüthszustand*) of the speaker is related to the condition or inner disposition from which the text arose. When this kind of empathic reading takes place, the original coherence of text and topic is discovered, and a more perfect form of religious speech results.[36]

As for the question of choosing texts, the natural answer seems to be: from the whole Bible. This presents several difficulties on further reflection. First of all, Catholics and Protestants have different canons with respect to the apocryphal literature. Would it be acceptable for a Protestant pastor to preach on an apocryphal text? Perhaps so, Schleiermacher answers, but since much of the literature is apocalyptic, its images are not terribly helpful for Christians. And the speaker must not forget that "hearers live in the image." Thus, these books should seldom form the basis for sermons in the evangelical church. Second, there are problems involved in relating the Old Testament to the New. In general, evangelical preachers should always prefer a New Testament text. There are several reasons for this. The New Testament sees Christ as the end of the law. Therefore, to speak from an Old Testament text is to assume a "historical starting point" and creates a foreign consciousness that is not the Christian consciousness of God. There is a difference between the Old Testament material that the New Testament authors themselves quoted and recognized as true expressions of Jesus' mission, and other Old Testament texts. The former can be used in Christian preaching quite well, but the latter can be used only more or less as mottoes, and this is always an inferior way of dealing with texts. For example, Schleiermacher says, Psalm 139 speaks elegantly of God's omniscience and omnipresence—ideas that are part of the Christian God-consciousness. But it puts these concepts in a legalistic framework totally alien to the Christian idea of redemption. Therefore, to base a sermon on this text the speaker would have to rip those concepts, as mottoes, out of the integrity of the text's own argument. One might argue that some Old Testament language in fact enters the Christian consciousness. But it usually has to do either with the general handling of worship (natural religion and morals) or with the legalistic mentality, which Schleiermacher takes to be "a certain anxiety, a diseased condition, a false outlook about the whole course of the religious consciousness." And there can be no argument that the speaker must first sketch this background for his hearers: that would be a matter for religious education rather than worship.[37]

Producing coherent religious speech involves the speaker in a "dialogue" between his life in his congregation and his immersion in the text of scripture. Schleiermacher is quite clear that both partners of this dialogue must be present for a successful outcome. The speaker must be so involved with his congregation that he can think their thoughts before them. At the same time, the speaker must also be a careful scholar whose ministry cannot be imagined "without a diligent occupation with the Bible . . . [that becomes] the center of all combinations of thought." Schleiermacher takes up and rejects a number of ways of distinguishing types of coherent topics and texts. Some people distinguish between intellectually persuasive (*unterrichtende überzeugende*) and moving or stimulating (*bewegende*) sermons. But really only the latter type have the genuine character of religious speech. Others distinguish between dogmatic and moralistic sermons. But this is an impossible separation, since in the religious impulse itself there is no feeling that does not pass over into activity. Finally, some distinguish between historical and didactic texts of scripture. But this is an imperfect distinction for religious speech, since both types of texts arise from religious impulses and ways of acting. Even what purports to be history is "only a religious impulse, that is, only the presentation of a way of acting that emerged from the religious consciousness in a particular case."[38]

> The historical can only have its purpose in that it is taken didactically, and the didactic in that it is traced back to life and the historical. The difference is that a historical text presents a single case, while a didactic text presents a general principle.[39]

### The Arrangement of Religious Speech

As Schleiermacher moves on to discuss the arrangement of sermons, his tone becomes much more practical. The questions really are: Do sermons need outlines? and, Should outlines be included in sermons? For the purposes of my argument, I simply wish to highlight several points he makes in this section. The important thing to keep in mind when organizing religious speech, he tells us, is that it is rhetorical. "The rhetorical organization relies on the fact that in each moment something happens for the effect [on the hearers], in each moment what one wishes to represent is contained, and not even hints of something are presented that could only be understood through what followed them."[40] Therefore, each individual part of religious speech must be both intellectually persuasive (*überzeugende*) and ethically moving (*bewegende*). Each part of the sermon must contain both concepts (dogmatic ideas) and moral incitements. Finally, each part of the sermon must show how the individual determination of Christian consciousness that is being discussed relates to the whole religious self-consciousness. Some people have argued that this requires every sermon to contain a complete system of theology, or at least some handy formula for one, such as the doctrine of the Trinity. But Schleiermacher denies both the possibility and the desirability of such a method. All religious speech *presupposes* an entire system of doctrine, but it can never (within humane time limits) *present* that system. Even more important, though, is that religious speech must be living representation (*lebendige Darstellung*) and not dry formulas (*trokkenen Formeln*).[41] The language of dogmatics must be translated to the language of the pulpit.[42]

### The Invention of Religious Speech

The invention (*Erfindung*) of individual thoughts that make up religious speech is the process of a dialectic between experience and reflection. The speaker should lose himself in the continuity of religious life, but should also take time to reflect on it. Religious speech ideally emerges from this meditative process. But there is a conflict between the speaker's need to settle on an outline and complete the sermon, and his need to remain open to what experience reveals even at unlikely moments. The speaker, then, must be careful to control involuntary thoughts that might interfere with his introspection, while yet paying attention to what might have caused them to arise. There are really only two kinds of failure in the invention of religious speech: failure sufficiently to express what is in oneself, and failure to exclude elements that have no place in religious speech.[43]

What if such careful introspection leaves the speaker without any ideas? Schleiermacher argues that more thought about the text itself is required. As for the "help books" that generate sermon examples, they are useless for authentic religious speech, where the content must develop in life experience. "The more sermons arise from sermons, the more estranged they are from the immediacy of religious life, and therefore the more dead they are," Schleiermacher argues, "and the best *auto da fé* would be to submit all these help books to the fire."[44] In fact, too many illustrations do not really improve a sermon. The specificities of an example will not be applicable to the majority of hearers, and so they will easily dismiss not only the illustration but the point behind it. If an example is to be fruitful, the hearer must take in the universality of it and at the same time find his special individuality in it. The best form of illustration, therefore, is the picture (*Bild*), because it has a relative universality. And the example is a proper element of religious speech only if it has a biblical character. The sermon does not achieve this biblical character by a mere accumulation of citations or repetition of biblical language. Rather, religious speech must be carried through in connection with its text, and every thought within it must have a biblical foundation.[45]

## The Expression of Religious Speech

A consideration of rules for the expression or delivery of religious speech makes up the final section of the theory. Much of this material is extremely pragmatic and technical. Schleiermacher considers questions ranging from the relative merits of preaching in local dialects versus high German, of reading versus memorizing sermons, and of learning from actors about how best to use gesture and facial expression in preaching.[46] For my purposes, I wish to single out just four points.

First, Schleiermacher insists that religious speech must be prose, not poetry. The precise definition of the distinction between prose and poetry must be borrowed from general literary theory, and it will change from time to time. But regardless of definitions, if one opts to follow the usual style of composition that characterizes prose—the alternation of short clauses and complex phrases—one is unlikely to wander into the realm of poetry. Poetry finds its place in worship in the hymns of the church.[47]

Second, Schleiermacher argues that the language must be *popular* throughout, that is, it must be the language of the congregation. All congregations, even the most cultured, contain unlearned people (*plebeje*), and religious speech would leave them untouched if it spoke only the language of the cultivated. Similarly, technical language, such as that of philosophy or theology, is ruled out.[48]

Third, Schleiermacher suggests repeatedly that "communicative representation" (*mittheilende Darstellung*) must be a personal act. For this reason, preachers finally cannot learn much from actors. "The preacher [*Geistliche*] is not less than an actor in what he does; but what makes an actor an actor does not qualify a preacher to be a preacher. For a preacher must always be himself, and an actor must deny himself and be another."[49] The speaker must thoroughly embody and personify the Word.

Finally, Schleiermacher insists that the best analogies for religious speech are drawn from everyday life. The sound of the voice, the nature of gesture and expression, should be the same as those used in "earnest intercourse and dialogue." It is not the grandiosity and pathos of the stage, but the quiet conversation before the fire, to which the speaker should aspire. The theory of religious speech ends with the warning that absolute rules in these matters are difficult to produce, since gesture and expression are culturally defined.[50]

The *Practical Theology* goes into much greater detail about the nature of religious speech than do the earlier texts we have considered in this chapter. But it only adds flesh to the skeleton of a theory Schleiermacher seems to have thought through as early as the 1790s. Religious language, also in the *Practical Theology*, is rhetorical, representational, and reciprocal or dialogical. With this fuller explication of his theory of religious language firmly in mind, we are now in the position to analyze his theology of preaching as it is developed in the *Glaubenslehre*.[51]

## PREACHING AS INCARNATIONAL EVENT

While Schleiermacher is quite clear about what he means in describing religious speech as "rhetorical," and why he believes it must be reciprocal or dialogical, the *Practical Theology* does not sufficiently explain what he means by "representation" (*Darstellung*). For more on this concept we must turn back to the *Glaubenslehre*. Already in the introduction ( §§ 1–31) to this work, Schleiermacher sets forth two fundamental principles that give us tools for unpacking the concept. In his discussion of the essence of Christianity, he asserts: "The appearance of the Redeemer in history is . . . neither an absolutely supernatural nor an absolutely suprarational thing," and "there is no other way of obtaining participation in the Christian communion than through faith in Jesus as the Redeemer."[52]

The first of these principles is the presupposition for how Schleiermacher develops his Christology in part two. But at the same time, it is an abstraction from his understanding of the incarnation. If Jesus is truly human and truly divine, neither his humanity nor his deity must be sacrificed to the definition of his person and work. If the Redeemer's appearance in history were neither supernatural nor suprarational, his deity would be compromised, and we could expect that he was just another extraordinary religious leader and not the "one who is to come" (Matt. 11:3). But if the Redeemer's appearance is *absolutely* supernatural and suprarational, his humanity is destroyed, God's act in Christ appears to be arbitrary, and true regeneration of Christians appears an impossible goal.[53] Therefore, Schleiermacher seeks to develop Christology in such a way that, while his divine origin is never compromised, Jesus' person and work can be understood as fully human (i.e., as capable of analogy to other human persons and actions).

The second principle, about faith as the means of moving from the corporate life of sin to the corporate life of redemption, seems straightforward enough. But Schleiermacher is concerned to define faith correctly. Simply put, faith "relates the state of redemption, as effect, to Christ as cause."[54] That is, faith is the certainty one has that Christ has put an end to the state of his or her being in need of redemption. This certainty is what leads individuals to join the communion of Christians. Once someone has this experience, it can be presented to others and they in turn may be moved to have the same experience. That, Schleiermacher tells us, is really what *preaching* is all about. But the impression that others receive from preaching about Christ is actually the *same* impression that Christ's contemporaries received directly from him. Thus "the ground of unbelief is the same in all ages, as is also the ground of belief or faith."[55] Faith comes from preaching, and the whole process of coming to participation in the Christian communion can be summed up in two points: the witness or testimony and its effect.[56] Schleiermacher rejects the aids that are often adduced to incite faith in Christ (or even substituted for true testimony), such as miracles, prophecy, and inspiration. These, so far from producing true faith, actually presuppose it. No one who is not already convinced of Christ's redemptive efficacy will come to be persuaded of it by these means.[57]

The assertion that faith in Christ comes about in exactly the same way for all Christians is not without problems. Can one really say that the eye-witnesses of the life and preaching of Jesus came to faith in the same way as do Christians living nearly two thousand years later? Do not the first apostles have a clear advantage in being so close to the events of the life of Jesus? These difficult questions preoccupy Schleiermacher, not in one section only, but throughout the entire explication of the *Glaubenslehre*. His conviction, in short, is that if the faith of the apostles were, indeed, of a different character than our faith in Christ, then we would not be adherents of the same religion. The *witness* of the apostles, it is true, has a kind of pride of place in the Christian church; but their *faith* is no different from the faith of any other believer.[58]

The source of faith is the preaching of Christ (*Predigt Christi*), either Christ's own self-presentation or the preaching of Christ by others.[59] This preaching is a representation (*Darstellung*) that evokes an impression (*Eindruck*), and it is efficacious (*wirkende*). In order to unpack what Schleiermacher means by these terms, we must explore his understanding of the self-presentation of Christ as he develops it in the Christology of the *Glaubenslehre* (§§ 92–105), his understanding of the preaching of Christ in the church (§§ 115–135), and his account of its effect in the lives of individual Christians (§§ 106–112).

### The Self-Presentation of Christ

Schleiermacher argues that the doctrines of the person and work of Christ (or, as he prefers, the "dignity" and "activity") imply each other and are, therefore, inseparable.[60] The person of Christ, his dignity, consists in one fact, described in two ways: from the divine and the human perspective. In the Redeemer, the ideal (*Urbildliche*) has become completely historical. Thus, though he is like all other humans and shares their nature, the Redeemer is distinguished from them by the constant potency of his God-consciousness, which is a "veritable existence of God in him."[61] The ideality of Christ does not prevent him from developing in the same way as other human beings, nor does it allow him to escape the concrete elements of human existence that are determined by one's location in time and place. But only by virtue of his ideality can we account for the unique dignity of the Redeemer; and ideality alone renders him suitable as an example for all, in spite of his groundedness in a particular historical location.[62]

The work or activity of Christ is similarly described in two parts: his redemptive activity consists in the assumption (*Aufnehmung*) of believers into the power of his God-consciousness, while his reconciling work takes them into fellowship with his untroubled blessedness.[63] It is in this section of Schleiermacher's Christology that we find the most help in understanding what he took to be Christ's "self-presentation." All Christ's activity proceeds from the being of God in him, but its expressions are all conditioned by the form of his specific human life. His "assuming" activity, then, is a creative production of his person. It seeks to form in its objects the will to assume him into themselves, or simply to assent to the influence of his activity. The best analogy for this activity is the kind of formative power that a master or teacher exercises over disciples who willingly submit themselves to his or her influence. Christ's activity forms both the person and the world: it changes the individuals to whom it is applied, but it also implants a new vital principle into the human race that will eventually transform all of society.[64] All of this is achieved through effective proclamation or preaching (*wirksame Verkündigung*).[65]

Schleiermacher distinguishes between his understanding of Christ's activity, as "mystical," and alternative points of view which he calls the "magical" and the "empirical." The mystical view is so called because it acknowledges that there can be no proof, strictly speaking, that this influence of Christ on believers takes place; it is a fact of inner experience. However, the inner experience is expressed outwardly in the formation of a new community, and the community mediates the continuing influence of Christ. The magical view, on the contrary, asserts that Christ can have this inward effect on believers immediately, quite apart from the community of faith. And the empirical view limits Christ's influence to that of teaching and example, and does not acknowledge that he actually communicates his God-consciousness and blessedness to the community of faith.[66]

The activity of Christ is divided into three offices: prophet, priest, and king. The prophetic office, in essence, contains all three, for it is the office that includes Christ's work in teaching.[67] Schleiermacher does not want to reduce the understanding of Christ's teaching to the "empirical" view, which he explicitly rejects. Rather, the source of his teaching was "the absolutely original revelation of God in him"; and its content was the reproduction of his powerful God-consciousness, which enabled the assumption of others into his fellowship.[68] His teaching was connected to the total impression made by his being—it was an immediate expression of his person. Thus everything Christ did or said, in a sense, is the manifestation of his prophetic office. But that is only because Christ's person was transparent to the being of God in him. The priestly office includes Christ's obedience and his intercession with the Father for believers. And the kingly office consists in Christ's provision of everything that the community of believers requires for its well-being.[69] Schleiermacher asserts again in his discussion of the threefold office that Christ's activity on behalf of believers is always and everywhere the same. There is no distinction, in other words, between that activity in the life of the earthly Jesus and that in the life of the church. "For even his original effect [*Wirken*] was purely spiritual; and, just as now his spiritual presence is mediated through the written Word and the picture [*Bild*] it contains of his being and effect, even so the original was mediated by his bodily appearance [*Erscheinung*]."[70]

## The Preaching of Christ in the Church

If the foundation of a community is essential to Christ's "mystical" communication of his God-consciousness, it seems appropriate to turn first to Schleiermacher's discussion of the church before examining his soteriology.[71] He divides his ecclesiology into three main parts: the origin of the church, the church in antithesis to the world, and the consummation of the church. What he has to say about preaching falls especially in the first two parts of the exposition.

The doctrines that explain the origin of the church—election and the communication of the Holy Spirit—are, in essence, abstract attempts to account for the *effect* of preaching. Just as Christ's incarnation was the beginning of the regeneration of the entire human race, so the erection of a permanent place for the preaching of the gospel among a people is the beginning of that people's regeneration.[72] The divine Word and Love, which seek human salvation, while always the same in themselves, only manifest themselves in history under concrete and particular conditions. So the Redeemer, the incarnate Word, was born in "the fullness of time," according to the divine decree of salvation. Similarly, individual people and nations only receive the Word, incarnate in preaching, in a particular place and time, and not everyone receives it at the same time. This leads to an apparent disparity among humans that must be accounted for by the doctrine of election. Election is a way of reconciling God's immutable will for salvation with the scandal of particularity that occurs under the conditions of finitude.[73] Similarly, the doctrine of the communication of the Holy Spirit attempts to describe *what* is communicated or effected by preaching—namely, union in the fellowship of believers, participation in the Holy Spirit, and living communion with Christ (which are really three different names for the same thing).[74]

The church in antithesis to the world is characterized by some essential and invariable features (scripture, ministry, sacraments, power of the keys, and prayer) and some features that are changeable and destined to disappear (plurality, fallibility). The invariable features of the church reflect and carry on Christ's activity and can similarly be divided among three offices. For the purposes of my argument, I shall focus on the church's reflection of the prophetic office of Christ: the doctrine of scripture and, especially, the doctrine of the ministry of the Word.

Building on the understanding of faith that he has already developed, Schleiermacher argues that scripture cannot be the foundation for faith in Christ. Rather, it is an expression of the faith of the authors and communities that produced it.[75] This does not mean, however, that scripture is only one among many expressions of faith. On the contrary, it has a normative role in the Christian community because it stands nearer to the "purifying influence of the living memory of Christ" than do later expressions of faith. Although scripture serves as a norm, this means neither that every later representation (*Darstellung*) of Christian faith must be uniformly derived from the canon, nor that it must contain at least the kernel of any future presentation. Since the Spirit has been poured out on all flesh, no age is without originality in Christian thought. But no later representation will be deemed truly Christian if it cannot be harmonized with scripture, and no others will have an equal authority in guaranteeing the Christian character of a representation of faith.[76]

But what of the ministry of the Word? Here we come to the heart of Schleiermacher's theology of preaching. Preachers, like Christ, exercise an efficacious influence on their hearers. Their speech arises, as did the Redeemer's, from the disparity in the strength of God-consciousness in themselves and others. They are active in communicating, and others are receptive in being influenced by, their self-presentation. While preachers truly speak of themselves—their own inner experience—they do not preach themselves or attribute the gifts that they communicate to themselves. Rather, their communication is the transparent medium through which their hearers encounter the living Christ.[77] In part all Christians share in the ministry of the Word, the duty to bear witness to their encounter with Christ.[78] But the public ministry of the Word is set apart as the duty of duly appointed ministers, in order to preserve order in the church and to ensure the powerful effect of the Word in the world.[79] What is important to note here is how carefully Schleiermacher draws the analogy between the work of Christ and the work of ministry. In fact, it is not too strong a statement to say that these two are actually one and the same. Christ, through his servants, communicates himself—the Word made flesh—through the efficacious influence of their self-presentation.

## Subjective Reception of the Preaching of Christ

How, then, do believers receive this activity of Christ? Schleiermacher describes this phenomenon in his soteriology. Chiefly, the reception of Christ's work can be summarized in two doctrines, corresponding to the redeeming and reconciling activities of Christ: regeneration and sanctification. Regeneration involves both a changed relationship to God (justification) and a changed form of life (conversion). Once believers possess living communion with Christ, more and more they submit their natural abilities to him, and so begin to live a life akin to his perfection and blessedness; this is what is meant by sanctification. It is primarily in his discussion of conversion that Schleiermacher describes the believer's experience of receiving Christ's self-presentation.[80]

Conversion is usually an ongoing process with no clear beginning or end. It involves regret, a change of mind, and an incorporation into the self of a feeling of blessedness. But what causes these changes to occur in one who is to be converted? Schleiermacher asserts that it is an "intuition [*Anschauung*] of the perfection of Christ."[81] Now if our conversion and the conversion of the apostles must have come about in the same way, then we must seek the common element in them. And this, quite simply, is *the Word*, taken in the sense of the entire prophetic activity of Christ. The only difference is that "the self-presentation of Christ is now mediated through those who preach him; but since they are dedicated to him as his instruments, the activity proceeds from him and is really his own."[82] In fact, it is impossible to give a single example of conversion apart from the mediation of the Word. It is the Word that influences hearers to feel the need of redemption and the satisfaction of that need in Christ.

> The efficacy [*Wirksamkeit*] of Christ's influence, then, is only in the human communication of the Word, but only in that this communication carries forward the Word of Christ and the indwelling divine power of Christ himself. This perfectly agrees with the truth that, in the consciousness of a person in the grip of conversion, every human intermediation disappears, and Christ is realized as immediately present [*vergegenwärtigt*] in his entire redeeming and reconciling activity, from the prophetic to the kingly office.[83]

The human Word that so renders Christ present is both supernatural and natural, both divine and human. The Word arises from the being of God in Christ, but it only expresses itself in the concrete particularity of human life.

Preaching, then, itself is analogous to the person of Christ: it is human and divine, historical and ideal. Hearers of the preached Word, under the appropriate conditions, encounter not a feeble human speaker but the Redeemer himself. In this sense, preaching is a re-presentation of the self-presentation of Christ. Its purpose is to make contemporary (*vergegenwärtigen*) the encounter with Christ that is the source of faith for Christians in all times. Of course, there is no magic formula for making this happen. At best, one can describe the conditions that are conducive for producing such an "incarnational event." First, clearly, it must happen in the community of believers. This Schleiermacher interprets broadly enough to include more than institutional church services. But yet, the private encounter with the Bible in the study could never become an incarnational event.[84] Second, the sermon must be biblical, that is, appropriate or adequate (*gemäss*) to the presentation of Jesus in the New Testament. Third, the sermon must arise out of the preacher's own intimate experience with the living Christ: it must be intensely personal, while yet allowing Christ to shine through. The preacher's personality must be the prism through which the being of Christ is refracted. Finally, the sermon must be apprehended in faith through the power of the Spirit. Even when everything is right with the presentation, the Word becomes flesh only according to the divine decree for the working out of salvation in history. When every aspect of the preaching event corresponds to these requirements, one can expect nothing less than the incarnation of the same Word that drew the first disciples to Jesus.[85] Thus, Schleiermacher's theory of religious speech is developed, at least in part, to explain the phenomenon of Christian reconciliation. Religious speech is reciprocal, he argues, because reconciliation through Christ occurs in community; it is rhetorical, because reconciliation occurs through a powerful and efficacious *influence*; and as representational language, religious speech actually presents what it speaks of—in the case of Christian language, the very presence of the Redeemer.

Like Calvin, Schleiermacher sees the preached Word as the best instrument for communicating the presence of Christ, as the primary means of grace. But, as we shall see in chapter 6 below, Schleiermacher took Calvin's concept of sacramental Word a step farther. He asked what the notion of the Word as the means of grace implied for the doctrine of the person and work of Christ. And his commitment to the sacramentality of the Word drove him to revise christological doctrines that Calvin left untouched in their patristic and medieval forms.

## NOTES

1. *Das Leben Jesu* (SW I/6:38–44, 238–39); cf. D. F. Strauss, *The Christ of Faith and the Jesus of History: A Critique of Schleiermacher's Life of Jesus*, trans. and intro. Leander E. Keck (Philadelphia: Fortress Press, 1977), 38–47; Johannes Wendland, *Die religiöse Entwicklung Schleiermachers* (Tübingen: J.C.B. Mohr, 1915), 181; Giovanni Moretto, "Angezogen und belehrt von Gott: Der Johannismus in Schleiermachers 'Reden über die Religion,'" *Theologische Zeitschrift* 37 (1981): 267–91.

2. The two epigraphs to this chapter allude to this view of preaching (*Schleiermachers Sendschreiben über seine Glaubenslehre an Lücke* [hereafter cited as *Sendschreiben*], ed. Hermann Mulert [Giessen: Töpelmann, 1908], 34; and *Gl.*, § 116.2). Cf. *Aus Schleiermachers Leben in Briefen*, ed. Ludwig Jonas and Wilhelm Dilthey (Berlin: Reimer, 1860–63), 4:335.

3. *KD* §§ 284, 285 (109–10; ET, 99–100).

4. *Friedrich Schleiermachers Reden über die Religion*, ed. G. Ch. Bernhard Pünjer

(Brunswick: C. A. Schwetschke & Son [M. Bruhn], 1879), 8–9, 195–96, 203–07 (ET, 82–83, 172, 178–80). Hereafter cited as *Reden*. Pages following ET refer to the English translation of the *Reden*, 1st ed. (1799): *On Religion: Speeches to Its Cultured Despisers*, trans. Richard Crouter (Cambridge: Cambridge University Press, 1988). See the discussion in Trillhaas, *Schleiermachers Predigt*, 6–11. Cf. Karl Barth, *The Theology of Schleiermacher: Lectures at Göttingen, Winter Semester of 1923/24*, ed. Dietrich Ritschl, trans. Geoffrey W. Bromiley (Grand Rapids: Wm. B. Eerdmans Publishing Co., 1982), 245–47; Christoph Meier-Dörken, *Die Theologie der frühen Predigten Schleiermachers* (Berlin: Walter de Gruyter, 1988), 13–25.

5. "I ask, therefore, that, disregarding everything that is usually called religion, you direct your attention only toward these individual intimations and feelings that you will find in all expressions and noble deeds of inspired people" (*Reden*, 24 [ET, 92]). Schleiermacher does not think authentic religious communication will always be heard (*Reden*, 148 [ET, 142]), nor does he think the true preachers of religion can impose their beliefs on others, since the very character of preaching is not didactic or doctrinal but expressive. Nevertheless, there is something "infectious" about authentic religious communication (*Reden*, 181–85 [ET, 163–65]).

6. *Reden*, 181 (ET, 163).

7. *Reden*, 181–82 (ET, 163).

8. *Reden*, 181 (ET, 163).

9. *Reden*, 150 (ET, 143). Cf. the later discussion of religious discipleship: "There are individuals to whom thousands attach themselves, but this attachment is no blind imitation and they are not disciples because their master has made them into this; he is rather their master because they have chosen him as that" (*Reden*, 152 [ET, 145]). See also his *Serm. Gal. 2:16–18* (SW II/2:651). The idea of an active receptivity to communication can be found in Schleiermacher's earliest writings. See, for example, *Vermischte Gedanken und Einfälle (Gedanken I)*, no. 147–48 (KGA I/2:34–35).

10. As narrator in the *Speeches*, Schleiermacher says of himself, "I . . . am . . . convinced to speak by an inner and irresistible necessity that divinely rules me" (*Reden*, 2 [ET, 78]). Later in the same text he states: "That I speak does not originate from a rational decision or from hope or from fear, nor does it happen in accord with some final purpose or for some arbitrary or accidental reason. It is the inner irresistible necessity of my nature; it is a divine calling; it is that which determines my place in the universe and makes me the being I am. Even if it were neither suitable nor prudent to speak of religion, that which compels me stifles with its heavenly power these small reservations" (*Reden*, 4 [ET, 79]). Cf. *Reden*, 9–10 (ET, 82). Schleiermacher's understanding of the compulsion to expression may owe something to romantic notions of creativity in which the artist's production is the outward expression of an inner drive (*Trieb*). However, Schleiermacher also believed this was a biblical concept, based on 2 Cor. 5:14. See, for example, his use of this text in *Serm. Gal. 3:21–23* (SW II/2:34); *Serm. Gal. 2:16–18* (SW II/2:652); *Serm. 2 Cor. 5:17–18* (SW II/2:729).

11. *Reden*, 9–10 (ET, 82–83).

12. Meier-Dörken argues that the church's preaching is not, according to Schleiermacher, this ever-repeated variety of mutual communication, but rather a vicarious representation of religious experience for those who do not have it. Thus it is destined to disappear. I do not find his interpretation of the text on this point convincing (*Die Theologie der frühen Predigten Schleiermachers*, 13–18, 273–75).

13. *Reden*, 11 (ET, 83); cf. *Serm. Luke 2:41–49* (SW II/4:274).

14. *Reden*, 215–16 (ET, 188). Schleiermacher thinks the ideal church is best represented by the prophecy of Jer. 31:33, alluded to by Jesus in John 6:45, "They shall all be taught by God." In this ideal community, every person becomes a mediator for others, because each one's unique individuality reflects the incomprehensible and infinite image of God differently. But there are no longer "religious virtuosi" who are more adept at representing the divine than others. See Moretto, "Angezogen und belehrt von Gott," 267–76.

15. *Reden*, 184–86, 215–16, 219–20 (ET, 165–66, 187–88).

16. See his early definition (September 27, 1797) of rhetorical speech in *Vermischte Gedanken und Einfälle (Gedanken I)*, no. 20 (KGA I/2:11).

17. The term is *"darstellend."* For more on this aspect of Schleiermacher's theory of religious language, see Wilhelm Gräb, "Predigt als kommunikativer Akt: Einige Bemerkungen zu Schleiermachers Theorie religiöser Mitteilung," *Internationaler Schleiermacher Kongress Berlin 1984*, ed. Kurt-Victor Selge, in two part-volumes, Schleiermacher Archiv, vol. 1 (Berlin: Walter de Gruyter, 1985), 2:652–59.

18. *Reden*, 185–86, 192, 209, 216 (ET, 166, 170, 182, 188). The mutuality of religious language makes it an action that forms community. In this sense, Schleiermacher's view of communication is a harbinger of recent developments in critical social theory. For a discussion of these relationships, see Günther Wenz, "Verständigungsorientierte Subjectivität: Eine Errinerung an den Kommunikationstheoretiker F. D. E. Schleiermacher," in *Habermas und die Theologie*, ed. Edmund Arens (Düsseldorf: Patmos, 1989), 224–40.

19. See note 16 above.

20. For example, Schleiermacher's *Weihnachtsfeier* (1806) may be seen as an explication of his view of religious communication. See Dawn DeVries, "Schleiermacher's Christmas Eve Dialogue: Bourgeois Ideology or Feminist Theology?" *Journal of Religion* 69 (1989): 169–83. It is interesting that the 1st edition of the *Glaubenslehre* does not contain the equivalent of §§ 15–16 in the 2d edition. Schleiermacher adds these propositions, in the context of a whole new organization of the Introduction, to an explicit section on the relation of dogmatics to Christian piety. See *Der christliche Glaube (1821/22)* (KGA I/7,1:9–121). It seems the question of the nature of dogmatic language was one of the least understood aspects of the 1st edition of the *Glaubenslehre*. See Schleiermacher's response to criticisms by J. Fries (*Sendschreiben*, 59–61). However, §§ 1–4 of the 1st edition contain seeds of the distinctions we find in §§ 15–16 of the 2d edition (KGA I/7,1:9–18).

21. *Gl.*, § 15.2 (ET, 77–78).

22. *Gl.*, § 16.1 (ET, 78–79).

23. *Gl.*, §§ 15.2, 16.1 (ET, 77–79).

24. *Gl.*, § 16.1,3 (ET, 78–79, 80–81).

25. *Gl.*, § 16.Zusatz (ET, 81–83).

26. KD, §§ 284–85.

27. Schleiermacher lectured on practical theology ten times, from the summer semester of 1812 through the summer semester of 1833 (*Schleiermachers Briefwechsel [Verzeichnis]*, 307–30). He did not, however, himself prepare the manuscript of these lecture notes for publication. The text of the *Practical Theology* as we have it in the *Sämmtliche Werke* was prepared by Jacob Frerichs from several handwritten manuscripts of Schleiermacher's lecture notes and eleven sets of notes taken by students who attended Schleiermacher's lectures in 1821/2, 1824, 1826, 1828, and

1833. In order to render a readable text, Frerichs opted to blend the sources and simply to note in the text where a particular passage was found in Schleiermacher's manuscripts. Unfortunately, we still await a critical edition of the *Practical Theology*, and Frerichs' *Verschmelzung* of the various manuscripts presents problems for interpretation, as he himself admitted (*Die praktische Theologie nach den Grundsätzen der evangelischen Kirche im Zusammenhange dargestellt*, ed. Jacob Freirichs [Berlin: Reimer, 1850], hereafter cited as *PT* [SW I/13:viii–ix]). Nonetheless, the *Practical Theology* remains a crucial source for understanding Schleiermacher's theory of religious communication, and it has been widely cited by other scholars. In my treatment of the text, I am not as interested in the precise wording or the arrangement of the material as in the substance of the ideas presented. One other point needs to be mentioned here: Schleiermacher gives the same subtitle to the *Practical Theology* that he gives to his *Glaubenslehre*, "nach den Grundsätzen der evangelischen Kirche im Zusammenhange dargestellt." As in the *Glaubenslehre*, he is attempting here only to draw together a synthesis of practical theology for a specific church in a specific place: the Evangelical Church of the Prussian Union. Thus, even when Schleiermacher claims to be offering a broader or more comprehensive discussion of a topic, it is still only intended to account for the subject as viewed in his own church. Cf. Trillhaas, *Schleiermachers Predigt*, 6–18; Wolfgang Steck, "Der evangelische Geistliche: Schleiermachers Begründung des religiösen Berufs," *Internationaler Schleiermacher Kongress Berlin 1984*, ed. Kurt-Victor Selge, Schleiermacher Archiv I.i–ii (Berlin: Walter de Gruyter, 1985), 717–70, esp. 742–62.

28. *PT* (SW I/13:83).

29. *PT* (SW I/13:76, 252).

30. Schleiermacher prefers the term *Geistliche* to *Prediger*, and this does not translate directly into English. "Clergyman" sounds far more institutional and ecclesiastical, and also has overtones of hierarchy that Schleiermacher would reject in principle (see his *Serm. Eph. 4:11–12* [SW II/2:692–709]). I have chosen to render it as "speaker" simply to be consistent with the language of religious speech. But Schleiermacher sees the *Geistliche* in worship in much more exalted terms than the word "speaker" suggests. The *Geistliche* is the one who breathes spirit and life into the words of the sermon and, consequently, into the souls of his hearers (see *Serm. John 13:34* [SW II/3:470–82]). In this sense, I think his choice of term is more than purely conventional. I will also use sex exclusive language in referring to the speaker, since Schleiermacher argued that women should not preach in public worship (*Gl.* § 134.1).

31. *PT* (SW I/13:201, 216).

32. *PT* (SW I/13: 203–4, 205, 213).

33. *PT* (SW I/13:206, 204, 207–11).

34. *PT* (SW I/13:217–18, 220, 232–34; cf. 229).

35. *PT* (SW I/13:235). Cf. Schleiermacher's remarks about the necessity for empathy in the interpreter of texts in his *Hermeneutics* (Friedrich Ernst Daniel Schleiermacher, *Werke: Auswahl in vier Bänden*, ed. Otto Braun and Johannes Bauer [Leipzig, 1927–28; reprint, Hamburg, Felix Meiner, 1967], 4:135–206, esp. 153–63).

36. *PT* (SW I/13:235–36).

37. *PT* (SW I/13:236–39). Cf. *Gl.*, §§ 128–32 (ET, 591–611).

38. *PT* (SW I/13:248; 240, 241, 242, 245–46, 247).

39. *PT* (SW I/13:247).

40. *PT* (SW I/13:257).

41. *PT* (SW I/13:256–58).

42. Cf. this passage from the *Sendschreiben:* "Dogmatic language is never designed to be carried over into the popular communication of sermon or catechism. In fact, it would be unwise to make this too easy. The necessity of translating [*verwandeln*] the expressions in which one receives these concepts into others guarantees a thorough thinking through and application of them, and we ought to expect this from our candidates for ministry" (*Sendschreiben*, 59).

43. *PT* (SW I/13:267–73).

44. *PT* (SW I/13:279–80).

45. *PT* (SW I/13:281–82).

46. *PT* (SW I/13:291, 310, 316).

47. *PT* (SW I/13:286–87; cf. 116–120).

48. *PT* (SW I/13:288–89).

49. *PT* (SW I/13:316).

50. *PT* (SW I/13:317–19).

51. It must be pointed out that the critique of Schleiermacher's theology of preaching in Barth's *Homiletics* is both inaccurate and unfair. He lifts out Schleiermacher's emphasis on preaching as an expression of religious experience, and the notion of a reciprocal or dialogical relationship between the preacher and his congregation, as if this were all Schleiermacher had to say about preaching. Then he asks: "Where is the Word of God in this immanent sea of feelings? Where is the ongoing seeking if all that is done is simply the expression of an inner possessing? What place is there for final waiting if the moving force is this-worldy possession or its lack, enjoyment or yearning? Not in any of these: Here is another world than that in which we are confronted by law and grace. It is another world than that in which God comes again and again. For it is the human world which as such flows out from itself and back into itself. . . . He then raises for us the question whether the Word comes from the congregation and whether it should not be viewed instead as the Word that comes to the congregation from outside" (*Homiletics*, trans. Geoffrey W. Bromiley and Donald E. Daniels [Louisville, Ky.: Westminster/John Knox Press, 1991], 22–23, 25). The brief extracts from Schleiermacher that Barth includes in this lecture are from the *Speeches on Religion* and the *Practical Theology*. To begin with, one cannot claim to have given a full account of Schleiermacher's theology of preaching without taking into account what he says in the *Glaubenslehre:* the *Speeches* do not provide a *Christian*, but a *religious*, theory of communication, and the *Practical Theology* is concerned more with technical than theological aspects of communication. But even in the *Practical Theology*, as I trust I have indicated above, Schleiermacher does not present preaching as an expression of merely immanent human emotions and relationships. Rather, as I assume Barth would agree, preaching is the interpretation of scripture to serve the Christian church in the present. The Word of God that comes from outside the congregation comes, for Schleiermacher no less than for Barth, *through* the encounter with scripture. Barth obfuscates their essential agreement on this point by quoting only snippets, out of context, with a different emphasis than they have in the original texts.

52. *Gl.*, §§ 13–14 (ET, 62–76).

53. *Gl.*, § 13 (ET, 62–68).

54. *Gl.*, § 14.1 (ET, 68–69).

55. *Gl.*, § 14.1 (ET, 68–69).

56. *Gl.*, § 14.3-Zusatz (ET, 70–76).

57. *Gl.*, § 16.Zusatz; cf. § 128.2 (ET, 81–83, 592–93).

58. *Gl.*, §§ 128–31 (ET, 591–608).

59. *Gl.*, § 128.2; cf. § 14 (ET, 592–93, 68–76).

60. *Gl.*, § 92 (ET, 374–76).

61. *Gl.*, §§ 93–94 (ET, 377–89).

62. *Gl.*, § 93 (ET, 377–85). It is interesting that Schleiermacher insists on ideality in order that the picture of Jesus will be a powerful example for all. Cf. his discussion of the *Bild* as the best kind of *Versinnlichung* (*PT*, 280–81).

63. *Gl.*, §§ 100–101 (ET, 425–38).

64. *Gl.*, § 100.2 (ET, 426–28).

65. *Gl.*, § 100.3 (ET, 428–31).

66. *Gl.*, §§ 100.3, 101.3 (ET, 428–31, 434–35).

67. *Gl.*, §§ 102, 103.2 (ET, 438–41, 442–46).

68. *Gl.*, § 103.2; cf. § 130.3 (ET, 442–46, 600–602).

69. *Gl.*, §§ 104–5 (ET, 451–75).

70. *Gl.*, § 105.1 (ET, 466–68).

71. The organization of the *Glaubenslehre* is tightly woven, according to methodological principles laid out in the introduction ( §§ 15–31). In some ways, logically, ecclesiology should precede soteriology according to Schleiermacher's own account of the phenomenology of faith. But for him, the doctrine of the church is composed of propositions of the third type, i.e., "utterances regarding the constitution of the world," and so belongs after an account of the consciousness of redemption in propositions of the first type, "descriptions of human states" (*Gl.*, § 30).

72. *Gl.*, § 116.2 (ET, 534–35).

73. *Gl.*, §§ 114.2, 118.1 (ET, 530–32, 539–42).

74. *Gl.*, § 124.1 (ET, 574–75).

75. *Gl.*, § 128 (ET, 591–94).

76. *Gl.*, §§ 129.2, 131 (ET, 595–96, 604–8).

77. *Gl.*, § 133 (ET, 611–14). This is why Schleiermacher insists that the ministry is "bound" by the Word of God in scripture (*Gl.*, § 135 [ET, 617–19]).

78. *Gl.*, §§ 133.2, 134; cf. §§16, 108.5, 127.2 (ET, 613–17, 78–83, 490–92, 587–89).

79. *Gl.*, § 134 (ET, 614–17).

80. *Gl.*, §§ 106, 107, 110 (ET, 476–80, 505–10).

81. *Gl.*, § 108.2 (ET, 483–87).

82. *Gl.*, § 108.5 (ET, 490–92).

83. *Gl.*, § 108.5 (ET, 490–92).

84. *Gl.*, §§ 134–35 (ET, 614–19); cf. *Serm. Luke 2:41–49* (SW II/4:266–81).

85. The incarnation of Christ is seen by Schleiermacher as a metaphor for the progress of spiritual life in individuals as well as in the human race as a whole. See *Gl.*, §§108.6, 109.3, 112.1, 116.2, 118.1, 120.1 (ET, 492–95, 499–503, 517–19, 534–35, 539–42, 552–53).

# 5

# SCHLEIERMACHER'S SERMONS
# ON THE SYNOPTIC GOSPELS

I am sure you will gladly testify, dear friends, that from the time you received the milk of the gospel in your first instruction in Christianity, right up until the present day, every such encounter with scripture was like a new, joyous, and powerful appearance of the Lord himself.
*Sermon on Luke 24:30–32*

The impression which all later believers received in this way from that which Christ effected—namely the common Spirit communicated by him and the entire Christian community, supported by the historical representation of his life and character—was just the same impression which his contemporaries received from him directly. . . . And so the source of unbelief is the same in all ages, as is also the source of belief or faith.
*The Christian Faith*

In spite of his preference for the Gospel of John, Schleiermacher spent a great deal of time thinking about the Synoptic Gospels. Between 1810 and 1833, he offered no fewer than eight lecture courses on Matthew, Mark, and Luke at the University of Berlin, and his four series of lectures on the life of Jesus naturally dealt extensively with the Synoptics. During the same period he taught two courses on the Gospel of John. Once, in the summer semester of 1821, Schleiermacher offered a course on the Passion narratives of all four Gospels.[1] In 1817, he published the first of what he projected to be a two-volume critical commentary on Luke-Acts.[2] (He never completed the second volume, on the Acts of the Apostles.) In the courses on hermeneutics and introduction to the New Testament, too, Schleiermacher dealt with the problems of interpreting the Synoptic Gospels. He considered thoroughgoing criticism of the Synoptics to be an urgent task for theology.[3]

But it was not only in the classroom that Schleiermacher faced the historical questions of the Synoptic Gospels. In the pulpit, too, he preached 185 sermons on the Synoptics that spanned the forty-two years of his work as a pastor. Taken together with the 129 sermons on texts taken from John's Gospel, these sermons represent slightly more than half of Schleiermacher's preaching activity. It would be a mistake, of course, to make too much of mere statistics, since we do not know to what extent the choice of text was limited by a lectionary.[4] But it is not insignificant that the last series of exegetical sermons that he chose to preach at the early services between August 1831 and February 1834 was on the Gospel of Mark.

We have explored Schleiermacher's concept of preaching as incarnational event.[5] His conviction that Christian religious language communicates the presence of the Redeemer arose from decisions about the nature of faith that are outlined already in the introduction to the *Christian Faith*. He argued that faith must always come about in the same way for all Christians, whether they are eyewitnesses of the events in Jesus' life or separated from those events by thousands of years. The source of faith is the proclamation of Christ, either his own self-proclamation or the representation (*Darstellung*) of him given in all Christian preaching.[6] The proclamation itself mediates Jesus' powerful God-consciousness, which draws the hearer into fellowship with his activity and life. Following the logic of Romans 10:17, Schleiermacher insists that "faith comes from preaching."[7] Therefore, preachers must so interpret the biblical texts as to draw out the "picture of Christ"[8] that is present in them and to allow it to influence those who are listening.

But what aspects compose that "picture of Christ"? This is the difficult question for the preacher, made even more difficult, perhaps, because of the shadow of doubt hovering over many of the purportedly historical events recounted by the Gospels. In this chapter, by looking at his sermons on the Synoptic Gospels, we shall examine the way in which Schleiermacher the preacher painted the picture of Christ. There can be no question that Schleiermacher was aware of the historical-critical problems associated with many of the Gospel narratives, since he lectured and wrote extensively on them. But what emerges from an analysis of his sermons is the remarkable independence of his preaching from these critical questions. The "picture of Christ" is composed of elements that are not open to historical verification.

It is necessary at the outset to state the principles by which some of the sermons are excluded from our attention and some are highlighted for more careful investigation. In his lectures on the life of Jesus, Schleiermacher divided Jesus' life into three periods: (1) before his public appearance, (2) from baptism to arrest, (3) from arrest to ascension. It was the second period, he believed, that should chiefly constitute the picture of Jesus, because this was the period of his free, influential activity.[9] This chapter's analysis of the sermons will follow Schleiermacher's periodization of the life of Jesus. Obviously it is impossible in the limits of a chapter to summarize the contents of all the sermons. Some are easily dismissed because, for Schleiermacher, they do not present historical problems. For example, it is unnecessary to discuss the substantial number of sermons on Jesus' discourses and parables.[10] Beyond that, the sermons chosen for extended analysis are selected because they are both representative of others and interesting in themselves. The reader will be directed to similar sermons and further examples of particular homiletic strategies in the footnotes.

## SERMONS ON JESUS' LIFE
## BEFORE HIS BAPTISM

In his critical work on the New Testament, Schleiermacher came to the conclusion that the stories of Jesus' birth and childhood were not historically reliable. "A report of the birth of Christ," he states in his *Life of Jesus*, "has no essential place in the gospel narrative, or otherwise it would not be missing from John and Mark."[11] Therefore, he concludes, "these events were altogether unimportant for explaining Christ's appearance or the beginnings of faith in him."[12] In the *Glaubenslehre* too, the narratives about Jesus' childhood are subjected to critical doubt, along with the christological doctrines that have been drawn from them.[13] As a pastor, however, Schleiermacher preached regularly at Christmas, and so was obliged to think through the meaning of these narratives for faith.[14] As we shall see, the historicity of the texts is never discussed in Schleiermacher's sermons. The stories are treated as if the events they record really happened.

In many of the sermons, Schleiermacher focuses his attention on a portion of the text that is poetic, such as the songs of Mary, Zechariah, and Simeon, or the angelic announcement to the shepherds.[15] This effectively averts historical questions, since it is the *content* of the message rather than the narrated events that is of interest. This is the strategy employed in Schleiermacher's 1831 sermon on Luke 2:10–11, entitled "The Redeemer's First Appearance: A Proclamation of Joy That Awaits All People."[16]

The sermon begins by emphasizing the already/not yet character of the angel's announcement: although the promised joy which shall be to all people is clearly in the future tense, the event on which it is founded has already happened. When we examine the scene of Christ's first appearance, we strive in vain to see there the signs of a joy of historical importance to the world. But our faith as Christians presupposes that already at his first appearance Christ was the Son of God, the Word made flesh. The angel's announcement gives us a clue about how we should celebrate Christmas: we should move from what has already happened to what has yet to come, from the past to the future. Thus, the sermon is divided into two main parts. In the first, the proclamation of Christ's appearance is considered as the archetype of a joy that we can have in the future; in the second, it is shown how the faith that grasps this future joy is the only assurance available in the face of all the anxieties we have about our future.[17]

The angel's announcement to the shepherds reminded them of the Old Testament prophecies about the Messiah; it did so intentionally. But if they had fixed their attention solely on that reference to the past, it is not likely that they would have grasped the gospel in faith. So much of what they expected on the basis of these prophecies would be missing from the scene that encountered them.[18] All prophecies about the future—whether

Old Testament, New Testament, or even our own images of the future—
are only uncertain representations. Just as the shepherds did not know
*how* the babe in the manger would fulfill his mission as the Christ, so we
do not know how the church will consummate its mission in the world.[19]

Someone might argue that if our joy in the future can only attach to such
uncertain images, it completely loses its worth for us. But, Schleiermacher
maintains, everything we can know about the future has only one truth
for us, and belongs to the blessings of our life only if it agrees with our in-
nermost longing and brings us peace. We do not know what happened to
the shepherds after they returned to their flocks. Perhaps they forgot all
about what had happened to them. But shortly after our text, we are told
of Simeon, whose whole life had been spent in longing for the Redeemer.
Although he was not permitted any clear picture of the future, his joy was
complete because his longing was fulfilled. And the same is true of us. We
can have joy in the future only if we are longing for something the Lord
can develop within us in that future. We must be seeking and striving for
his salvation, for peace between God and humanity.[20] Then his promises
give us joy in our future.

Our comfort and joy in the future, however, are entirely a matter of
faith, just as our understanding of what happened in the past comes to us
through faith.[21] The angel gave the shepherds a sign to demonstrate the
truth of his proclamation. But what a dubious sign! Unless they had already believed that such a Savior was to be born, the sign would never
have convinced them. And that is always the way it is: "Faith alone can
hold on to joy in the form of the Redeemer, a joy that shall be not only to
all the people, but also to the entire human race."[22] When the Redeemer
himself taught on earth and went around doing miracles, only faith received his wonderful works as proofs; those who did not believe persis-
tently misinterpreted his words and deeds. That is why the apostle Paul
said that the preaching of the gospel was a stumbling block to the Jews
and folly to the Greeks; they were both lacking the faith by which they
could grasp the future in the present. If the shepherds had faith, then,
when they returned to their flocks, whenever they had worries or anxieties about the future they would have reminded themselves that the Messiah had come and they had seen him.

When *we* have anxiety about our future, when we see that good is not
triumphing over evil, or that much of what we are trying to achieve seems
to be failing, the source of these worries is always unbelief. But if we truly
believe that the Savior is born *for us,* then we cannot be led astray about
the future. We will remember that everything for which we thank and
praise God can be summed up in what we have done in the name of the
Lord—those deeds in which he became *present* to us. This experience,
Schleiermacher tells us, "repeats itself in every significant [human] rela-

tionship," and it is the "key for everything that has happened in the period from when the Redeemer first appeared on earth to the present
day."[23] That is, our joy in the future, like the shepherds' joy, is based on a
faith that has "seen" the Redeemer—"seen" him wherever he has become
present for us. And this is assurance enough that the heavenly light
streaming out from this divine child will indeed one day totally penetrate
the darkness of this world.[24]

Schleiermacher's exegesis of the angelic announcement is certainly
fairly involved. But, interestingly, he is not particularly concerned with
the history of the nativity. The shepherds do appear in his interpretation
of this text, but only insofar as they are hearers of the same angelic promise
that we receive. Any particular questions about them as people (including
the kinds of questions a historian might ask) are ruled out from the beginning. It is the Christ present through the Word that he emphasizes.

A somewhat different method of dealing with the text is used in
Schleiermacher's 1831 sermon on Luke 2:15–20, entitled "The Diverse
Ways in which the Proclamation of the Redeemer Is Received."[25] The activities of the characters in the narrative are scrutinized for what they can
reveal about the nature of faith. The sermon is divided into two main sections. In the first, Schleiermacher considers these diversities of reception
of the gospel in themselves, while in the second he considers their relationship to the current form of Christian fellowship. There are only very
few Christians who receive the gospel as did the Virgin Mary and "ponder all these things in [their] heart." More are like the shepherds, who did
not deny the testimony of the angels and went out of their way to see
whether what they had been told was true. But, without a doubt, most
people are like those who wondered at what the shepherds told them.[26]
We might think that the reason for these various reactions is the extraordinary event of Christ's birth itself. But Schleiermacher begins by showing that in ordinary human affairs, whenever something new is announced the same types of reactions occur.

Having established the homogeneity of Christian experience in the
Gospel narratives and common human experience in the world as we
know it now, Schleiermacher returns to the story of the text. We ought not
to be quick to judge either the "wonderers" or the "shepherds" for their
weakness of faith. Those who wondered had every right to be suspicious,
given all the messianic pretenders that were current at the time. And their
wondering itself shows that they at least had an open mind. The Redeemer
might have said of such people what he said of another on a different occasion: "He who is not against us is for us."[27] Similarly, although we do
not know whether the shepherds ever became Christ's disciples, we must
not be too quick to judge them. They perhaps never had the opportunity
to see Jesus again, or else, if they did, perhaps they did not connect him

with the one for whom they praised God on the night of his birth. We cannot blame them if they did not come into a closer relationship with the Redeemer, for in their own way they were bearers of the Word.[28]

There are many among us in the church today, Schleiermacher argues, who are "wonderers." They see that the Christian religion has sprung from a very unlikely source and has grown to influence many nations, but yet it does not really change the lives of those who profess it as one would expect it to. And there is some truth in such skepticism, for "much greater things ought to have happened in the human race through the fellowship [of believers], had only the relation of Christians to Christ been stronger and closer."[29] We can answer the skepticism of these wondering brothers and sisters by telling them that it is only human weakness and confusion that has prevented the powerful working of the church within the human race. The very issues these wonderers raise contain the seed of a true enjoyment of God's kingdom.

The "shepherds" in our church are those who "diligently inquire about the stories [*fleissig forschen nach den Geschichten*] to which Christian faith attaches itself, and make divine revelation the object of their reflection."[30] Schleiermacher notes that these in their own way receive the gospel, test it, confirm it through their inquiry, and then spread the Word to others. Yet what we often hear about them is that they are lacking the most important part of piety—the silent pondering that one observes in a Mary. But just such "shepherd" types are responsible for maintaining the purity of the Christian witness; through their inquiry, the Holy Spirit reforms the church.

When he finally turns to Mary, Schleiermacher highlights the ambiguity of her position. It was in no way remarkable that she, who had already had a personal visit from an angel, should ponder all these things in her heart! But was her faith true and blessed faith already then? Was not Mary slow to believe the divine message of her Son? With Mary and all people of the "Marian type," it is important to remember that their faith also contains the seed of unbelief; that their confirmation in faith is also a work carried out gradually over a period of time; and that in them too the Word must be ever anew enlivened to movement and growth.[31] The conclusion is that we must all work together, each receiving and communicating the Word in the way that he or she best can. Only in this way will it become clear that the Savior who was born is not the Savior of a handful of individuals alone, but of the entire world!

In this sermon Schleiermacher draws his hearers into the Gospel history by asserting the homogeneity of Christian experience in the past and in the present. His concern is much more with the present meaning of the text than with questions concerning the historicity of the events it records. The events are simply taken as given, but they do not hold interest for

Schleiermacher. Rather, he tries to disclose the inner disposition (*Gemüths-zustand* or *Gesinnung*) of the characters in their relationship to the Redeemer. The birth narratives were included in the Gospels, Schleiermacher believed, not to record accurately the outward circumstances of Jesus' conception and birth, but rather to tell the reader something about the way Christ was first received in faith.[32] This is not a matter of historical curiosity, however, but of vital interest to all Christians whose faith must arise in just the same way.

Thus it should not be a surprise that the same Schleiermacher who, on his own testimony, "skeptically" dismantled the narratives about Jesus' childhood on historical grounds[33] could, on January 7, 1821, begin a sermon as follows:

> My friends in Christ! There is but little information about that which, in our Gospels, joins directly to the narrative of the birth of our Lord and Redeemer and holds our attention on the early days of his life. But this scanty information is so rich in significance that I decided to make it the subject of our morning meditations this year until Lent.[34]

The series he announced that morning comprised five sermons that bear many similarities in the interpretative strategies they employ. We shall look briefly at four of them.

The first sermon, "Longing for What Is Better," is on Matthew 2:1–12, the story of the visit of the Magi. Schleiermacher takes the sages as powerful symbols[35] of the longing for redemption. The sermon has two main sections: in the first, he considers the longing for what is better in and of itself, and in the second he looks at its relationship to Christ. The longing for redemption, Schleiermacher argues, is a by-product of the consciousness of sin, and all people have it to some degree—even those outside the Judeo-Christian traditions, such as the Magi. Certainly when this longing is missing, it is "the most tragic condition of human nature."[36] While this first section of the sermon offers some profound observations about human existence under the reign of sin, it says virtually nothing about the characters in the text. Section two asserts that only Christ can satisfy this deep longing for redemption. Again, the Magi and their journey are taken as apt symbols of this truth. The star that guided their journey came to rest only where the newborn Redeemer lay. "So, too, the longing of the human heart does not rest until it has found him."[37] And like the Magi, believers will find peace only when they simply desire to be with the Redeemer, and not always to test his claims to authority.[38]

The story of the slaughter of the innocents (Matt. 2:16–18) is treated similarly. Schleiermacher takes Herod's wicked command as a symbol of the sin of holding back the progress of Christianity.[39] But the narrative of the text is not treated merely as a symbolic point of departure. The first section of the sermon wrestles with the problem of theodicy: How can we reconcile ourselves with the death of these innocent babies? The text reports an event, presumed to be historical, that is morally problematic. The preacher, it seems, is obligated to address problems of this nature directly, and Schleiermacher does so. The details of his answer need not concern us for the moment.[40] What is interesting is that Schleiermacher refuses simply to allegorize a "historical" narrative that presents a challenge to the goodness of God. We shall return to this point later.

The fourth in this series of sermons, on the story of the Holy Family's flight into Egypt, once again uses the historical narrative as a point of departure for conveying some rather complex theological concepts. The first section of the sermon discusses the flight to Egypt in relation to divine providence. It could seem to have been a miscalculation on God's part that Mary and Joseph should have to flee Bethlehem with such a tiny baby in their arms. Would the Redeemer of the world survive? Schleiermacher's answer to these rhetorical questions is perhaps surprising: God planned the escape to Egypt so that people would have faith in Jesus based on the proper foundation. If Jesus had stayed in Bethlehem, people would undoubtedly have heard of the marvelous signs that accompanied his birth, and they would have been tempted to believe in him because of the miracles. So, too, in Bethlehem there were many who were familiar with the Old Testament prophecies about the coming Messiah, like Simeon and Anna, and the word would surely get around that Jesus was the fulfillment of those prophecies. But miracles and prophecies cannot ground true faith in the Redeemer: only the total impression he makes on those to whom he appears can create this faith.[41] God, then, wisely removed Jesus from a place where many would have come to a superficial faith and had him return to a different region, where his miraculous origins would be unknown.

The second part of the sermon takes Joseph's problem as an example of the ambiguity of moral reasoning. Joseph wanted to be a good father and provider for his family. Fleeing to Egypt might seem a drastic course to pursue. If he had asked the advice of friends, they might have discouraged him from putting so much importance on what was essentially a bad dream. But Joseph knew that he was following God's will. And this is what every Christian must continuously seek. Absolute rules do not always represent God's will, but we can be confident that God will show us the right way if we are seeking for it.[42] In both parts of the sermon, Schleiermacher uses the narrative as a springboard for talking about the nature of faith in Christ.

A final sermon in the series looks at the story of the boy Jesus disputing with the rabbis in the Temple in Jerusalem. Schleiermacher thought the usual view of the story—that Jesus knew more than the rabbis and so was really teaching them—mistaken; he could see no support for it in the text.[43] Since this episode came from the time before Jesus was ready to assume his public teaching office, Schleiermacher found Jesus in some ways more comparable to all Christians in this story than he is later on. So Jesus' way of behaving in the Temple is taken as an example (*Vorbild*) of how Christians should behave in church. The first part of the sermon dwells on Jesus' enthusiasm for the Temple. This should convince Christians that life in the church is absolutely necessary. Who more than God's own Son could claim to have no need of instruction in God's law? Yet Jesus eagerly sought out opportunities to hear the scripture expounded. That is because preaching is the original form of the divine Word and the only one that brings faith. Moreover, in the gathered assembly of believers we can see God's Word through the prism of many individual personalities, and all these will enrich our understanding of it.[44] In the second section of the sermon, Schleiermacher notes that Jesus was not simply *present* in the Temple, but was actively engaged in asking and answering questions. This is taken as the example of how criticism of preachers should be undertaken, and also of a kind of active listening in which both hearers and preachers should engage during a sermon.[45]

While the details of this short narrative are carefully scrutinized, it is not with a view to discerning their exact historical anchoring. Rather, as in the other three sermons, Schleiermacher's entire interest is in the inward history of the present-day life of faith and its external supports. As his title betrays, the whole story is taken as an *example* of what Christian services of the Word should be like. This is a strategy of interpretation distinct from, but not dissimilar to, the allegorical method used in some of the other sermons in this series.

## SERMONS ON JESUS' ACTIVITIES
## BETWEEN HIS BAPTISM AND HIS ARREST

The discussion of Jesus' public life constitutes the heart of Schleiermacher's portrait of Jesus, in his *Life of Jesus* as well as in his preaching. Of the 185 sermons on the Synoptic Gospels, 146 deal with the period between Jesus's baptism and his arrest. Of these, it is those on texts about miracles that are especially problematic for the historian. Schleiermacher believed Jesus' public ministry was characterized by an external and an internal aspect. The external aspect included the time and location of Jesus' activities and also his miracle-working activity. The internal aspect included Christ's self-communication in teaching and in attracting others to himself and forming a community.[46] It is the internal aspect of Jesus' activity that forms the essence of his "picture," while the external aspect merely frames it or puts limits on it. In his preaching, therefore, Schleiermacher chose far more often to preach on Jesus' explicit teaching in parables, discourses, and the like; only some thirty sermons deal explicitly with miracle stories. Once again, in an effort to deal efficiently with these sermons, I will take clues from Schleiermacher's own categories in his *Life of Jesus* for dealing with the texts on which they are based. He distinguishes four kinds of miracles recorded in the Gospels: (1) those performed by Jesus on people, such as healings and exorcisms; (2) those performed by Jesus on inanimate objects, such as the stilling of the storm or the changing of water into wine; (3) those performed without Christ's will or intent, such as the healing of the woman with a hemorrhage; (4) those performed by God through the instrumentality of Jesus, such as the raising of Lazarus.[47]

For Schleiermacher the historian, not all categories of miracles are equally problematic. He is most confident of the essential historical core of healing miracles, because it is more possible to discover analogies to them in ordinary life and because they can be conceived as moral acts on the part of Jesus.[48] More difficult are the second and third categories of miracle stories. In fact, he states, some of these narratives when taken literally are simply incomprehensible.[49] The miracles in the last category, moreover, are simply irrelevant because they do not tell us something necessary for faith in Christ.[50] In what follows, I shall discuss a number of sermons representing each but the last of the four classes of miracle stories.

Schleiermacher preached four sermons on exorcism stories. The earliest, in 1810, was on Matthew's telling of the story of the Gadarene demoniacs,[51] and the other three were from his series of homilies (1831–33) on the Gospel of Mark.[52] The 1810 sermon examines the characters of the narrative for what they can reveal about faith in the Redeemer. The possessed men themselves are taken as symbols of the condition of humanity under the reign of sin. The demoniacs' affections are disordered: sensuousness (*Sinnlichkeit*) has complete control over them, so that even when the possibility for redemption is presented to them, they do not wish to receive it. However, the possessed men also represent the extent to which even humanity under the conditions of sin does not lose its sense for what is holy and divine (*Sinn für das heilige und göttliche*). For their question to the Redeemer, "Have you come here to torment us?" indicates a conviction that "the evil spirit that possessed [them] could not oppose the efficacious nearness of the Son of God."[53] The people of the region are represented as those who witness the powerful workings of the Word and yet resist its call for change—for a "new order of things"—instead of the familiar, if imperfect, order in which they live. The tragedy of their refusal to be changed by Jesus' preaching is witnessed by the actual horrors that they suffered shortly after his death: they lost everything they were trying to protect from change.[54]

The exegetical series of sermons on Mark are strikingly simple in comparison with many of Schleiermacher's topical sermons. They usually make only one or two brief points drawn directly from the text. In the homily on Mark 1:23–28, Schleiermacher tries to show how faith in the Redeemer is independent of the seemingly antiquated views of science that pervade the Gospels. Already in the early nineteenth century, people were questioning whether demonic possession was a real phenomenon or, rather, an ancient way of speaking about mental illness. Schleiermacher lays down a general rule that deciding about the facticity of demonic possession and other similarly problematic things in the New Testament is a matter entirely indifferent for Christians, so long as the view one holds maintains the saving power of Christ and his divine origin.[55]

In his sermon on Mark's narrative of the Gerasene demoniac, Schleiermacher addresses two main themes: first, the moral problem of the destruction of the herd of swine, and second, the effect of the presence of Christ on those around him. The story, simply taken as it stands, seems to reflect poorly on Jesus. But in fact the blame really rests with the people of the region, who let the sick man run with the swine and made no attempt to care for him. They should have foreseen the possibility of disaster.[56] The point of the story is to demonstrate the powerful effect of the Redeemer on individuals. Like the Gerasene demoniac, all Christians order their affections and preserve their sanity through efficacious communion with Christ.

The final sermon on an exorcism narrative is on Mark 9:14–29. Schleiermacher argues that it is essential to read this pericope in the context of what happened just before it. Jesus descended from the mountain with Peter, James, and John, only to find the other disciples engaged in a heated dispute with the Pharisees. The story of the exorcism is intended to show that only a certain *quality* of faith can produce the healing that characterizes the coming of God's reign, namely, faith possessing a circumspect, ordered, and peaceful state of mind. The disciples' passionate arguments had rendered them unable to be instruments of healing. This is what Jesus meant when he told the disciples that "only prayer can drive out this kind" of demon.[57]

Schleiermacher preached seven sermons on Jesus' healing miracles, six of them in the series of homilies on Mark.[58] He uses two main strategies in dealing with these texts: either he "demythologizes" the text (i.e., argues against a supernatural explanation of it), or he takes the healing event as a symbol of an aspect of Jesus' teaching. For example, in preaching on the healing of Peter's mother-in-law, he states at the outset:

> I would be very happy if everyone were to believe that this [story] is not
> in the strictest and most genuine sense of the word a miracle story. . . .
> Our Redeemer, to be sure, loses nothing if one more or less of the deeds
> he did is called a "miracle."[59]

If we presuppose, on the contrary, that this story records an event that happened in a perfectly normal way, we can get at the true meaning of the story: that is, the power of the will and love over the body. Peter's mother-in-law wanted to play her proper role as Jesus' hostess, but she could not do this without getting out of bed. The power of her will and her love for the Redeemer actually caused her fever to break. And this very ascendancy of the spirit over the flesh is what Jesus has given to the human race.[60]

Similarly, in preaching on Jesus' healing of a leper, Schleiermacher asserts that "the more this story depends on the extraordinary powers of the Redeemer, the less we can take it as an example for ourselves."[61] Rather, this story is about Jesus' compassion and the leper's confidence. The story of the healing of a paralytic who was lowered on a bed from the roof (Mark 2:1–12) is, likewise, about the power of the spiritual over the bodily. The man's body becomes healthy when he is overcome with the consciousness of forgiveness.[62]

When it was harder to "demythologize" a narrative, it seems, Schleiermacher turned to his other strategy of taking the miracle story as a symbol of Jesus' teaching. The healing of the deaf-mute (Mark 7:31–37) is taken as a symbol of the lack of receptivity in humans for the Word of God. Until the Redeemer unstopped the deaf man's ears, he was unable to speak or communicate. So too, until the Redeemer "opens" human beings and enables them to receive the Word of God, they are unable to speak the Word and communicate it to others.[63] Jesus' healing of a blind man in Bethsaida is considered along with the pericope that follows, containing the confession of Peter. The blind man, after Jesus' initial ministrations, could see but could not see clearly. This is a symbol of people's confusion about the identity of the Redeemer. Jesus points to this problem in his question to the disciples: "Who do people say that I am?" Like the blind man, these people will only be brought to see clearly through the nearness and aid of the Redeemer.[64]

Schleiermacher preached on both the Matthean and the Markan pericopes of Jesus' stilling of the storm. The treatment of Matthew 8:23–27 is the earlier of the two, preached in 1810, while the sermon on Mark 4:35–41 comes from 1832. The 1810 sermon bears the title "Confidence and Lack of Faith as Represented in Jesus' Boat Trip," and this title is an accurate clue to what Schleiermacher's approach to the miracle story will be. Instead of concentrating on the miracle itself, he is interested in the *Gemüths-*

*zustände* of the characters of the story, a technique we have already discussed above. Jesus' sleep is taken as a symbol of his absolute confidence in God. He knows that his vocation is not to sail the ship but to proclaim the gospel, and he has just finished performing that office in his sermon on the mountain. Now, overcome with weariness, Jesus goes to sleep, confident that God will care for everything else. This should be a model for our faith.[65] Schleiermacher contrasts Jesus' untroubled sleep of faith with the guilty sleep of Jonah the prophet, who slept, not in confidence, but as a means of escape from God's call and his vocation.[66]

The disciples, however, have a lack of faith (*Kleingläubigkeit*), and so the terrors of the wind and waves drive them to wake the Redeemer. They should have known that Jesus could not die before he had established his kingdom—they should have had confidence in God's providence, as Jesus did.[67] Perhaps they took the storm as a sign of God's disapproval and woke Jesus, as Jonah's companions woke him, to answer for himself. Then Jesus' reprimand makes perfect sense, for their faith had turned to unfaith. Schleiermacher draws the general conclusion from this that superstition (*Aberglaube*), which "regards the immediate result as a sign of divine good-pleasure or judgment," can turn faith (*Glaube*) into unfaith (*Unglaube*).[68]

We should learn from the disciples that we can be confident in the invincibility of the kingdom of God, even when it appears to be in danger or distress. Sometimes we are at risk of the same kind of unfaith as the disciples because we believe that we are indispensable—that we are the only ones left who can do God's work. But we will discover, as did Elijah, that there are many others through whom God is working to build the kingdom. Even the disciples were not indispensable; no, "God alone was and is and always will be indispensable in his Kingdom."[69] So we should rest secure in the knowledge that God will work his purposes out.

Schleiermacher turns to the miracle itself at the end of the sermon. He begins by contrasting the divine power demonstrated in the miracle with merely human abilities. This move is interesting, for it shows that, regardless of how he views the story as a historian, Schleiermacher does not question its factuality as a preacher. But the miracle itself is not of interest; rather, it is the doctrine that the miracle illustrates that is important. In stilling the storm, Jesus gave his disciples a sign that even the powers of nature exist only to serve the building of God's kingdom. Now, since God has given humans dominion over the earth, we are to use art and science to learn to control and direct nature, just as the Redeemer did here. But we must always do this remembering that building the kingdom is the goal. Schleiermacher ends by reminding his hearers that Jesus gives his disciples a promise that they too will do remarkable things: "You will cast out demons by using my name; you will speak in new tongues; you will tread on scorpions and they will not sting you; you will pick up snakes in your hands, and if you drink any poison it will not hurt you; and my power in you will be mighty to strengthen the weak and heal all the sick."[70]

The 1832 homily on Mark 4:35–41 is not as complicated as the earlier sermon. The main point Schleiermacher stresses is that faith in the ultimate victory of God's plan for reconciliation is what gives us equanimity in the toils and troubles of life.[71] It is Jesus' words of reprimand to the disciples that occupy him, and not the physical event of the miracle. What we can conclude from Schleiermacher's treatment of this miracle story is that, while the factuality of the account is not a question, neither is the miracle itself of particular interest. The stories are told to suggest the nature of true faith and the embracing reach of the kingdom of God. The history, as history, is simply irrelevant.

Schleiermacher preached only once on the story of the healing of the woman with a hemorrhage, in his 1831–34 series of homilies on Mark. He begins the sermon with the bald assertion that it is impossible to say much about the miracle itself because we cannot imagine how it could have happened. For us, however, it can be a symbol of how God has ordained some people to be active and others receptive in life: there is a reciprocity of giving and taking that is part of the order of things. Christ alone is in no need of receiving from others.[72] The story is about the longing for healing that is the prerequisite for salvation. The longing was created in the woman by Jesus' preaching, and when she finally realized that only he could satisfy this longing, she was healed. Jesus rightly identifies this as the result of faith. His question, "Who touched me?" shows that he valued the establishment of personal relationships—he did not help people in general, but only in intimate ties of relationship. And that is still how it is in the church and in society: the ties of personal relationships are necessary for true health.[73]

In this sermon Schleiermacher attends to the details of the narrative in order to discover what they say about saving faith, a faith we share with the woman of the story. The miracle is not explained, indeed, *cannot be* explained. But neither does it need to be. The significance of the story is not the miracle but the doctrine that it illustrates. As Schleiermacher states in the *Practical Theology*, "The historical can only have its purpose in that it is taken didactically."[74] For this reason, the very man who doubted the factuality of many of the miracle stories in his role as historian could preach on the stories as if they were true. Does that make Schleiermacher the preacher dishonest? Or is he simply following the same interpretative strategy that Calvin used in his sermons on the Gospels?

## SERMONS ON JESUS' PASSION
## AND RESURRECTION

We have already noted that Schleiermacher does not think the period after his arrest is constitutive to the life of Jesus conceived as a historical biography.[75] Christ's free influential activity comes to an end then. Nor does he believe that Christ taught that his death would have special salvific consequences. Rather, as Jesus states explicitly in John 13, it is the *Word* that he has spoken that makes the disciples clean. The forgiveness of sins is the effect of his preaching, and his death is only one moment in the course of an entire ministry. "Nowhere does Christ say that his death has some special and peculiar efficacy apart from his whole life."[76] And in the *Glaubenslehre,* Schleiermacher carefully dismantles atonement theories that attribute unique importance to Jesus' death.[77]

It is precisely in his treatment of the death and resurrection of Jesus that Schleiermacher receives the sharpest criticisms from Karl Barth and Hans Frei. For Barth, Schleiermacher is not in line with medieval and Reformation understandings of Christ's death. He does not take sufficiently seriously the depth of Christ's suffering; and he fails to see that it is the *death* itself, and not simply Christ's obedience, that brings about reconciliation with God.[78] Barth concludes, "The significance of Christ's death [for Schleiermacher] is simply that it is the summit of what man can do in relation to God when the human will is submerged in the divine will."[79] Frei criticizes Schleiermacher from a different angle: namely, that he fails to make sense of the narrative of Jesus' death because he concludes (in his lectures on the life of Jesus) that Jesus may not have really died. His interpretation is "unfitting, indeed ludicrous."[80]

In my analysis of some of these sermons, I want to show that the case against Schleiermacher's interpretation is not so easily made. At any rate, he does not preach on the narratives of Jesus' passion and resurrection much differently than did Calvin: they both move constantly from the history to doctrine. The material difference between their treatments of Jesus' death is that Calvin preaches the doctrine of substitutionary atonement, while Schleiermacher does not.

Schleiermacher preached only twenty sermons on the Synoptic accounts of the time between Jesus' arrest and his ascension into heaven. Because he is so clear about his conviction that Jesus' true office is to present or proclaim himself (and *through* himself his Father), Schleiermacher stresses repeatedly in these sermons the content of Jesus' *proclamation,* rather than the external facts of his death, resurrection, and ascension. These events are simply part of the whole ministry of Christ on earth. These sermons also embrace the whole range of interpretative strategies that are by now familiar to us: the texts are seen as exemplary, as allegories or symbols, as expressions of inner dispositions, or as summaries of doctrine.

Schleiermacher seems to have interpreted scripture as an example for Christian instruction more often in the sermons he preached early in his career (before 1809).[81] In a very early sermon, from 1794, he interprets the disciples' disbelief at the women's testimony to Jesus' resurrection as an opportunity to discuss "Lack of Faith Regarding Things from the Other World."[82] He begins by stating that we are in the same position as the disciples with respect to the story of Jesus' resurrection: we do not have access to a *proof* of it. And from the text he draws the conclusion that there are both good and destructive kinds of doubt. It is good doubt not to take human imagination for divine revelation, or to go against the rule of conscience.[83] But it is destructive doubt that only believes what is perceptible to the senses. We are to live by faith, not sight.[84] The narrative of Jesus' crucifixion is treated in a similar fashion in a sermon from 1799: "Some Feelings of the Dying Jesus That We Should Hope for in Our Last Moments."[85] Jesus' cry of dereliction was an indication that he was sad to leave his work on earth when so much was left to do. And this is how we should approach our death.[86] Jesus did not pay attention to the unfair judgment he received from those around him, and neither should we.[87] And Jesus died surrounded by his beloved friends, and renewed in ties of love and community. This too is what we should hope for.[88]

Like Calvin, Schleiermacher was not beyond using allegorical interpretation when it suited him. In a sermon from 1830, "Observing the Circumstances That Accompanied the Last Moments of the Redeemer," Schleiermacher interprets the darkness that fell at the time of the crucifixion in this way.[89] The darkness was not just a coincidental eclipse of the sun: it was an extraordinary sign, which demonstrated the mysterious connection between nature and spirit. It symbolizes the darkness—error, insanity, and sin—of those who crucified Christ. But even more significant, the reappearance of the sun was a sign that, because of God's gracious decree, never again would the light of salvation disappear from the world.[90] The rending of the curtain in the Temple is a symbol of the end of a special priesthood and of the beginning of a full disclosure of God's will to humanity.[91]

An entire Easter sermon is based on an allegory that Schleiermacher borrows from Paul.[92] He looks at Luke's account of the empty tomb as a symbol of what our "resurrection life" of faith is like. We share Christ's death and resurrection in baptism—even its mysterious and inexplicable aspects. The narrative begins with an empty tomb, not an account of when or how Jesus was raised. So, too, the beginnings of our spiritual life are hidden in impenetrable darkness.[93] Although he pursues this allegorical interpretation to the end of the sermon, Schleiermacher interrupts himself briefly to take on the question of the miracle of the resurrection itself:

> Since the time we began to look more into the historical aspect of the Kingdom of God, it has been much questioned and debated whether the Resurrection of our Redeemer—the most elevated and important of what we call wonders—happened naturally or supernaturally. . . . When we read, "Christ was raised through the glory of the Father," we are all filled with the impression that this was an extraordinary, special revelation of the glory of the Father, not connected with any other or comparable to something else. . . . It shall always remain the glory of the Father through which Jesus was raised from the dead. And if we ask after what happened with him, in him, and around him, between his death and his resurrection, then we are troubling ourselves over something for which no explanation is given, and for which, indeed, none is needed.[94]

This is a characteristic move for Schleiermacher and one we have seen him make in his sermons on miracle stories. But it is remarkable that in 1832 he dared to apply it to "the most elevated and important" of miracles. It is important to notice, however, that he does not question the historicity of the resurrection story: on the contrary, he seems to take it for granted. But what exactly happened is simply not of historical interest to him.

We have already seen many examples of sermons where Schleiermacher uses the narrative to reveal the *Gemüthszustände* of characters in the story, and he uses the same technique in these sermons. The second half of a sermon already discussed (on Luke 23:44–49) talks about the effect of the events at the crucifixion on the hearts of those who witnessed it. The proclamation of the death of Jesus, the picture of his crucifixion, are powerful instruments communicating grace. A man like the Roman centurion was enabled, through witnessing the spectacle of Christ's death, to make a confession of faith. And those who had sought to execute the Redeemer now beat their breasts and went away. This may have been the preparation they needed for receiving the grace of the gospel later from the apostles' preaching.[95] In an 1810 Ascension Day sermon, Schleiermacher considers Jesus' parting words to the disciples for what they reveal about their faith.[96] Jesus left them a reassurance of his authority, because their confidence in his power may have been shaken.[97] He calls them to proclaim the gospel, because they had not yet been able to do this in the complete purity of faith.[98] And he promises the disciples his continuous presence with them, a spiritual presence that will keep them steadfast in faith.[99] Schleiermacher ends each of the three sections of the sermon with a statement of the homogeneity of Christian experience: we are like the disciples, our needs and weaknesses are the same as theirs.

One could give many examples of sermons on these narratives that turn from history to doctrine. I shall mention just a few. In 1821, Schleiermacher preached a series of sermons on the seven last words of Christ. His word to the thief on the cross, "Today you will be with me in Paradise," is taken as a springboard for discussing the nature of eternal life. It does not mean escape from death, or even life after death. Rather, eternal life is the state of being in the presence of the Redeemer. The thief who received this gift at the very end of his life had no less than disciples who had followed Jesus their whole lives.[100]

The cry of dereliction presents a peculiar problem for Schleiermacher, because it could seem to represent a disturbance in Jesus' untroubled God-consciousness.[101] But if we recognize that Jesus is simply quoting the words of Psalm 22, this gives us a different perspective. The psalmist was not anticipating his immediate death when he spoke these words. And neither was Jesus singling out his death with special horror. No, Jesus surely had the whole psalm in mind when he spoke these words, and Psalm 22 ends with a statement of confidence in God's plan and praise for God's goodness.[102] Schleiermacher agrees entirely with Calvin: in spite of his real suffering, the Redeemer's faith was never shaken.

Jesus' last word, "Father, into your hands I commend my spirit," is also a quotation from a psalm, Schleiermacher notes. The psalmist was not thinking about his death when he spoke the words; in quoting this passage, Jesus is demonstrating that for him there is no real difference between his life before and after death. And because Jesus assumes us into his communion with the Father, we can have the same confidence in the continuity of life.[103]

A final doctrinal sermon I want to mention is the sermon for Easter Monday, 1824: "The Connection Between the Effects of Scripture and the Immediate Effects of the Redeemer."[104] Schleiermacher takes the story of the appearance of Christ to disciples on the road to Emmaus as a springboard for talking about the relationship between Word and sacrament. Jesus' explanations of scripture are like the preaching of the Word in the church, and his breaking of bread with the disciples is like the Eucharist. Both Word and sacraments are necessary—they were necessary for the disciples back then, and they are for us today. The Word clarifies the connections between things, it convicts us of sin and opens the door to encounter with the Redeemer. But the sacraments are like Christ's immediate physical presence: they open our eyes, renew our memories, make our hearts burn within us. In this sermon, Schleiermacher graphically demonstrates how the Christ of the Gospel history is the same Christ of the church's preaching and sacraments.

## PREACHING AND THE PROBLEM OF HISTORY

In the foregoing analysis, we have discovered that Schleiermacher almost never mentions historical difficulties in his sermons. The probability or improbability of angelic visits, miracles, and even the death and resurrection of the Redeemer is never taken up. In fact, on the rare occasions when historical questions are raised, it is to highlight their inconsequentiality for faith. That is not to say that Schleiermacher discounts these events; on the contrary, he almost always speaks as if he presupposed their essential actuality. But neither does he dwell merely on the words and events of the narratives as if they were a truth in themselves. The Gospel stories are taken as examples, allegories, symbols, expression of consciousness, poetic expression of doctrine—all of which require the preacher to transfer the text from past to present, to say not so much what the stories *meant*, as what they *mean*. Above all, the New Testament is an encapsulation of the first representation of the preaching of Christ. Thus, in his sermons on the Gospels, Schleiermacher tries to make that preaching of Christ transparently clear—so clear that his hearers will be confronted, as it were, by Christ himself.

In spite of material differences in their interpretation of the texts, Calvin and Schleiermacher have remarkably similar homiletic strategies. Neither is particularly curious about the history behind the texts, although both of them seem to presuppose the historicity of the events narrated. Neither of them can bear to say only what the words and narrative structure of the text would permit, for they both constantly translate their texts from stories to general principles, doctrine, or applications to present experience. And both preachers state explicitly that the proclamation conveys not mere information about Christ, but the very presence of the Redeemer himself.

Did it make a difference to Schleiermacher the preacher that, as a historian, he thought it improbable that Jesus stilled the stormy sea, or that Jesus may not have really died on the cross? Apparently not. But here is where there may be a genuine parting of the ways with Calvin. For to Calvin the atonement, at least in part, hinges on the historicity of a transaction between God and the God-man that culminates in Jesus' death and resurrection. Schleiermacher, on the contrary, formulates the work of Christ in such a way that it can always be understood to be accomplished through the preaching of Christ.[105] It is to these issues that we must now turn our attention.

## NOTES

1. *Schleiermachers Briefwechsel (Verzeichnis) nebst einer Liste seiner Vorlesungen,* ed. Andreas Arndt and Wolfgang Virmond, Schleiermacher-Archiv, vol. 11 (Berlin: Walter de Gruyter, 1992), 295–330.

2. *Ueber die Schriften des Lukas: Ein kritischer Versuch* (Berlin: Reimer, 1836), SW I/2:v–220. ET, *A Critical Essay on the Gospel of Luke,* trans. Connop Thirlwall (London: John Taylor, 1825).

3. *Das Leben Jesu* (SW I/6:239); cf. *Ueber die Schriften des Lukas* (SW I/2:12–13).

4. Wolfgang Trillhaas, *Schleiermachers Predigt,* expanded 2d ed. (Berlin: Walter de Gruyter, 1975), 22.

5. The first epigraph to this chapter demonstrates how Schleiermacher thought of preaching. The "encounters with scripture" he has in mind are actually preaching events–gatherings of the community to hear scripture expounded (SW II/2:190).

6. The second epigraph to this chapter is one of the places in which Schleiermacher articulates this principle (*Gl.,* § 14.1 [ET, 68–69]). Cf. *Gl.,* § 128 (ET, 591–94).

7. *Gl.,* § 14.3, §§ 100–101, § 105.1, § 108.5, § 121.2 (ET, 70, 425–38, 466–68, 490–92, 562–64).

8. Schleiermacher uses the term *Bild Christi* frequently, and others like it that are visual metaphors for the object of faith. "All Christian piety depends upon the appearance [*Erscheinung*] of the Redeemer" (*Gl.* § 29.2). "For even his original effect was purely spiritual; and it was mediated through his physical appearance [*Erscheinung*] in just the same way as even now his spiritual presence is mediated through the written word and the picture [*Bild*] it contains of his nature and effect" (*Gl.,* § 105.1). "May the divine Redeemer be born in us, so that we become like him and grow ever more able to appear in divine form. And to that end, holding fast to this holy picture of him from the moment it first appeared to us, let us adore the divine Child, the Savior of the world, that the picture may grow and increase in us and our entire being be formed in likeness to him" (*Sermon on Phil. 2:6–7* [SW II/2:573–74]). The picture owes its existence to the stirring self-presentation of Christ which is now "mediated by those who preach him; but they being appropriated by him as his instruments, the activity really proceeds from him and is essentially his own" (*Gl.,* § 108.5).

9. *Das Leben Jesu* (SW I/6:45).

10. Schleiermacher was not troubled by the question of recovering the actual sayings of Jesus. He regarded the presentation of Jesus' words in the Gospel of John to be a reliable historical source, and he used it to determine what might be actual words of Jesus in the Synoptic Gospels (*Das Leben Jesu* [SW I/6:274–80]; cf. *Einleitung ins neue Testament,* ed. G. Wolde [Berlin: Reimer, 1845], in SW I/8:315–44, esp. 332).

11. *Das Leben Jesu* (SW I/6:58).

12. *Das Leben Jesu* (SW I/6:70). Cf. *Ueber die Schriften des Lukas* (SW I/2:15–37), and *Einleitung ins neue Testament* (SW I/8:263–67).

13. *Gl.,* § 97, § 103.2.

14. Interestingly, among Schleiermacher's published Christmas sermons, only nine of eighteen are on the birth narratives of Matthew and Luke.

15. See, for example, his sermons on Luke 1:31–32 (SW II/2:55–68); Luke 1:44–55, 67 (SW II/7:557–65); Luke 1:78–79 (*Ungedruckte Predigten Schleiermachers aus den Jahren 1820–1828*, ed. Johannes Bauer [Leipzig: M. Heinsius Nachfolger, 1909], 74–81. Hereafter cited as Bauer [1909]). Luke 2:14 (Bauer [1909], 82–83); Luke 2:25–32 (SW II/7:117–34); and Luke 2:28–35 (SW II/4:432–41).

16. SW II/3:132–42.

17. SW II/3:134.

18. SW II/3:135.

19. SW II/3:136.

20. SW II/3:138.

21. SW II/3:139.

22. SW II/3:139.

23. SW II/3:141.

24. SW II/3:142.

25. SW II/2:329–42. This approach to the text must have been a favorite of Schleiermacher's because he used much the same outline twice before: in 1794 (Bauer [1909], 83–85) and 1802 (Bauer [1909], 86–87).

26. SW II/2:330–31.

27. SW II/2:334.

28. SW II/2:335.

29. SW II/2:337.

30. SW II/2:337–38.

31. SW II/2:339–40.

32. *Ueber die Schriften des Lukas* (SW I/2:19). In the *Glaubenslehre*, Schleiermacher makes this point about the New Testament in general: "Just as the original disciples' faith sprang from Christ's self-proclamation, so the faith of others sprang from the preaching of Christ by the Apostles and many more. The New Testament writings are such a preaching come down to us, and so faith springs from them too. But in no wise conditionally on the acceptance of a special doctrine about these writings, as having had their origin in special divine revelation or inspiration. On the contrary, faith might arise in the same way though no more survived than testimonies of which it had to be admitted that, in addition to Christ's essential witness to himself and the original preaching of his disciples, they also contained much in detail that had been misinterpreted, or inaccurately grasped, or set in a wrong light because of confusions of memory. . . . We have assumed . . . Scripture . . . only as expressing faith" (*Gl.* § 128.2–3).

33. *Das Leben Jesu* (SW I/6:69).

34. SW II/4:404.

35. As in chapter 3, when I use the word "symbol" in this chapter, I mean it in the common dictionary sense of something that stands for something else. When the symbolism is extended through a story, I refer to this as "allegory."

36. SW II/4:405–7.

37. SW II/4:410.

38. SW II/4:410–11.

39. SW II/4:442–55.

40. They will not, in any case, surprise readers familiar with his treatment of the problem of evil in the *Glaubenslehre*, especially *Gl.*, §§ 75–78.

41. SW II/4:750–58; cf. *Gl.*, § 14.
42. SW II/4:758–64.
43. *Gl.*, § 103.2; cf. *Das Leben Jesu* (SW I/6:78–79).
44. SW II/4:266–74.
45. SW II/4:275–81.
46. *Das Leben Jesu* (SW I/6:165–66).
47. *Das Leben Jesu* (SW I/6:206–14).
48. *Das Leben Jesu* (SW I/6:219–20).
49. *Das Leben Jesu* (SW I/6:221).
50. *Das Leben Jesu* (SW I/6:231–38).
51. *Serm. Matt. 8:28–34* (SW II/1:414–24).
52. *Serm. Mark 1:23–28* (SW II/5:43–53); *Serm. Mark 5:1–20* (SW II/5:232–44); *Serm. Mark 9:14–29* (SW II/6:11–23).
53. SW II/1:417–18.
54. SW II/1:419–21. This is one of many places in Schleiermacher's sermons where his interpretation of the Jewish people borders on anti-Semitism. The destruction of Jerusalem and the dispersion are seen as divine judgments on the Jews' rejection of Jesus.
55. SW II/5:43–48.
56. SW II/5:239–40.
57. SW II/6:11–23.
58. SW II/5:54–95, 394–401, 424–34; SW II/6:111–23; Friedrich Zimmer, "Predigtentwürfe aus Friedrich Schleiermachers erster Amtsthätigkeit," *Zeitschrift für Praktische Theologie* 4 (1882): 285–87.
59. *Serm. Mark 1:29–38* (SW II/5:55).
60. SW II/5:58. It is interesting to keep in mind that Schleiermacher preached this sermon in the fall of 1831, during a massive outbreak of cholera in Berlin, an epidemic that claimed the life of the great idealist philosopher G.W.F. Hegel (1770–1831).
61. *Serm. Mark 1:39–45* (SW II/5:70–71).
62. SW II/5:81–95.
63. SW II/5:394–401. This sermon is a powerful proof that Schleiermacher did not understand redemption to be a purely human possibility and achievement, as the neo-orthodox critics alleged. It is the Redeemer himself who creates the possibility for the reception of the gospel in a human heart. Barth's assertion, for example, that Schleiermacher in the last analysis understood redemption merely as strengthening, and the Redeemer only as a strong helper or a helping power, simply does not stand up to careful scrutiny ("Schleiermacher," in *Die Theologie und die Kirche* [Munich: Chr. Kaiser Verlag, 1928], 176).
64. SW II/5:424–34.
65. SW II/4:251, 254–55.
66. SW II/4:252. This sermon is somewhat unusual in that Schleiermacher draws a major part of it from an Old Testament narrative. It also has more allusions to Old Testament texts than do most of his sermons.
67. SW II/4:259.
68. SW II/4:257.
69. SW II/4:260–61.
70. SW II/4:263–64. This is a paraphrase of Mark 16:17–18.
71. SW II/5:228–29.

72. *SW* II/5:246–47.

73. *SW* II/5:250–59.

74. *PT* (SW I/13:247).

75. *Das Leben Jesu* (SW I/6:45–46).

76. *Das Leben Jesu* (SW I/6:348).

77. *Gl.*, § 104. Schleiermacher does not cite or discuss either Mark 10:45 or Matthew 20:28 in this proposition. But these passages could be taken to express a saving significance to the death of Jesus. Similarly, in his sermons on these texts, Schleiermacher does not regard Jesus' words about giving his life as a reference to vicarious atonement. Rather, they are interpreted along with the words that precede them ("The Son of Man came not to be served but to serve") as a statement about the kind of service that builds the kingdom of God. That Schleiermacher did not regard these words as having anything to do with the *unique* activity and dignity of the Redeemer is indicated by the fact that he urges Jesus' self-sacrificing love as a moral example for all Christians. He totally disregards the term "ransom" (*Bezahlung* or *Lösegeld*) in his interpretation of the text (*Serm. Matt. 20:20–28* [SW II/1:437–48]; *Serm. Mark 10:41–52* [SW II/6:110–23]); cf. the *Life of Jesus*, where he gives a similar explanation of the phrase *lutron anti pollōn* (SW I/6:346–47). See also § 99, where Schleiermacher argues that the facts of the resurrection, ascension, and second coming are not constitutive of the doctrine of the person of Christ. I discuss Schleiermacher's Christology more fully in chapter 6.

78. Karl Barth, *Die Theologie Schleiermachers*, 144–66. Interestingly, though, Calvin says, "The death and passion of our Lord Jesus would not have served anything to wipe away the iniquities of the world, except insofar as he obeyed" (*CO* 46:920; see p. 38 above).

79. Karl Barth, *Die Theologie Schleiermachers*, 166.

80. Hans Frei, *The Eclipse of the Biblical Narrative*, 313.

81. See Wolfgang Trillhaas, *Schleiermachers Predigt*, 56; cf. Karl Barth, *Die Theologie Schleiermachers*, 145–52.

82. *Serm. Mark 16:10–14* (SW II/7:218–28).

83. *SW* II/7:219–22.

84. *SW* II/7:225–26.

85. *Serm. Mark 15:34–41* (SW II/1:41–53).

86. *SW* II/1:44–45.

87. *SW* II/1:46.

88. *SW* II/1:49.

89. *Serm. Luke 23:44–49* (SW II/2:442–51).

90. *SW* II/2:444–45. Trillhaas speaks of this sermon in arguing that there is a kind of optimism in Schleiermacher's interpretation of the Passion. But it is interesting that Schleiermacher moves on immediately to say that there will inevitably be "dark times" in the progress of the kingdom. His "optimism" is based not on human possibilities, but on the invincibility of the divine decree of redemption (Trillhaas, *Die Predigt Schleiermachers*, 56–67).

91. *SW* II/2:446.

92. *Serm. Luke 24:1–3* (SW II/3:253–64).

93. *SW* II/3:254–55.

94. *SW* II/3:256–57. Trillhaas notes that in Schleiermacher's Easter sermons "so-called saving events withdraw" and are replaced by the total picture of Christ (*Die Predigt Schleiermachers*, 67).

95. SW II/2:448–50.
96. *Serm. Matt. 28:16–20* (SW II/7:411–18).
97. SW II/7:413–14.
98. SW II/7:414–16.
99. SW II/7:416–17.
100. SW II/2:123–37.
101. *Serm. Matt. 27:46* (SW II/2:399–416).
102. SW II/2:400–408.
103. *Serm. Luke 23:46* (SW II/2:151–60).
104. *Serm. Luke 24:30–32* (SW II/2:187–203).

105. I suspect that it may be Schleiermacher's understanding of the atonement, rather than his treatment of the Gospel narratives, that so irritates Barth and Frei about his interpretation of Jesus' death and resurrection.

# 6

# THE LIVING WORD AND
# THE WORK OF CHRIST

We must understand that as long as Christ remains outside of us, and
we are separated from him, all that he has suffered and done for the
human race remains useless and of no value for us.

Calvin, *Institutes of the Christian Religion*

Just as originally individuals were laid hold of by Christ, so even now
it is always through the work of Christ himself, mediated by his spiritual presence in the Word, that individuals are taken up into participation in the new life.

Schleiermacher, *The Christian Faith*

The suggestion that there are lines of continuity between Calvin and
Schleiermacher is often greeted with thinly veiled incredulity. Has not
that case been closed already, long ago? Barth asserted in 1922 that the line
running back through Kierkegaard to Luther, Calvin, Paul, and Jeremiah
most certainly did not include Schleiermacher.[1] But the evidence we have
seen above suggests that the case is not nearly as clear-cut as he assumed.
Calvin and Schleiermacher share remarkably similar understandings of
the Word of God—the very doctrine at the center of the neo-orthodox critique of Schleiermacher—and the task of preaching. And both Calvin and
Schleiermacher demonstrate a relative indifference to historical concerns
in their preaching. The Word of God, for each of them, refers primarily to
the incarnate Word, Jesus Christ, as witnessed in scripture and present in
preaching. The sermon does not merely point back to saving events that
happened in the life of the Jesus of history, but rather *itself conveys*, or is
the medium of, the presence of Christ in the church. Preaching is Christ's
"descent" to us, as Calvin puts it.[2] Both Calvin and Schleiermacher argue
that salvation is a work of the *Christus praesens*, who unites with believers
and shares with them all the benefits of his special relation to the Father.
But there are *some* differences between them, especially in how they relate
the doctrines of the sacramental Word and the work of Christ.

## CALVIN'S CHRISTOLOGY AND SOTERIOLOGY:
## A PROBLEM OF COHERENCE?

There is very little consensus about Calvin's Christology in the secondary
literature, and this is undoubtedly an accurate reflection of the complexity of his views. Ever the biblical theologian and humanist rhetorician,
Calvin seems to have delighted in gathering as many evocative metaphors

as possible under the umbrella of his treatment of an individual doctrine, even at the risk of contradiction. And nowhere is this more evident than in his Christology: Christ is prophet, priest, king, brother, sacrifice, substitute, example, victor, judge, and food.[3] The metaphors abound, and they suggest divergent directions for the doctrines of the person and work of Christ that may even be mutually exclusive.

While it is probably true, as John F. Jansen suggests, that "later Calvinism has too easily confined Calvin's doctrine of atonement to Anselmic terms," it is also true that the notion of substitutionary atonement was one of Calvin's central terms for the work of Christ.[4] And here we stumble upon a problem in Calvin's system: some of his christological metaphors in book 2 of the *Institutes* do not hold together well with his understanding of justification and sanctification in book 3, where the emphasis is on redemption through union with Christ. To state the problem bluntly: If Christ really took our place and satisfied our debt to God the Father, the satisfaction should be valid even if we do not believe it. A debt paid is a debt paid. But Calvin opens book 3 by asserting that everything Christ has done for the salvation of humanity would be *useless* if Christ were not to unite with those whom he wills to save.[5] This lack of coherence between Christology and soteriology in Calvin's system has been noted and commented on by others, and I am inclined to believe it cannot finally be resolved.[6] The interpreter tasting Calvin's rich blend of metaphors finally has to decide which of the many ingredients she or he finds dominant.[7]

I wish I could argue that, for Calvin, it is the *Christus praesens* that predominates in Christology. Certainly there is one chapter in which the work of Christ is mainly an ongoing one in the church—a work of the present Christ.[8] Calvin argues that Christ received his anointing as prophet, priest, and king not only for himself, but also to take us as his companions in these offices. The work of Christ is not only something *extra nos;* it is also *in nobis*. But on the whole, it seems, Calvin assumes the subject of Christology to be the Jesus of history, whose redemptive activity was a transaction with God that happened in his life, death, and resurrection. In *Institutes* 2.16 Calvin runs through the second article of the creed and explains in turn the salvific import of his birth, death, resurrection, and ascension, each event being presumed to be factual. Calvin's Christology, then, not only coheres badly with his soteriology, but despite the neglect of historical details in his sermons, it also entails historical claims that he would have found vulnerable to historical criticism had he ever had to face such challenges. One can only wonder how differently Calvin's Christology might have looked had he attempted to understand the work of Christ in connection with his doctrine of the sacramental Word.

## SCHLEIERMACHER ON THE PERSON
## AND WORK OF CHRIST

Schleiermacher set about describing the person and work of Christ in a different manner from Calvin. Although he asserts that any dogmatic system must establish its connection with language that has been recognized and approved by the church, he also maintains that "the ecclesiastical formulae concerning the person of Christ need to be subjected to constant criticism."[9] It is this dialectic between accountability to, and criticism of, tradition that characterizes his Christology, and it leads him to significant revisions of traditional formulas concerning the work of Christ.

Schleiermacher presupposed that faith comes about in the same way in all times and places: it is always the effect of the preaching of Christ, that is, the self-proclamation of Christ and its continuance in the church.[10] For this reason, he did not need, like Calvin, to accord a special salvific significance to all the individual events (or assumed events) in the life of the Jesus of history, which, if they occurred at all, are not as accessible to later believers in Christ as to the first eyewitnesses. Rather, he sought to understand the work of Christ in such a way that *all* believers would receive it through the same process. But how exactly is that?

A key passage for Schleiermacher's doctrine of the work of Christ is John 15:3: "You have already been cleansed by the word that I have spoken to you." In a sermon on this text, he contrasts these words with those of 1 John 1:7: "The blood of Jesus his Son cleanses us from all sin." He notes that, when Jesus spoke the words of John 15, he had yet to die, but nonetheless was able to assure the disciples that they were already cleansed from their sins. This means that Jesus' *Word*, and not some transaction between Jesus and God the Father that occurred in Jesus' death, is the actual instrument of reconciliation. Schleiermacher is careful to point out that Jesus' "Word" is not his teaching alone, as if the disciples were saved merely through information and education. Rather, the Word Jesus refers to is the totality of his self-presentation to the disciples, including his submission to death on the cross. This Word saves not by imparting information, but by uniting the disciples with Christ. Words, in general, are what make intimate human relationships possible. Jesus' Word, then, is the instrument that mystically unites him with the disciples.[11]

The contrast with Calvin on this point is interesting. In a sermon on Matthew 25:51–66, Calvin tries to account for the fact that Jesus stood silent before his accuser, the high priest Caiaphas. He concludes that Jesus' silence needs to be understood in connection with his assumption of a new office at the time of his trial—the office of Redeemer of the world. At first, after his temptations in the wilderness, Christ was sent as a *minister of the Word*, and during his public life he performed this office faithfully. But now, after his arrest, he has assumed the office of *Redeemer*, and so he voluntarily keeps silence and accepts condemnation in our place. He did not wish to escape death, for he knew that only through his death would he acquit us before God.[12]

Although Calvin speaks of the need for union with Christ, and of the proclaimed Word as the instrument of this union, he insists, nonetheless, that an objective, historical sacrifice of the God-man is the sine qua non of reconciliation. Schleiermacher, on the contrary, puts the Word itself at the center: the self-proclamation of Christ and its continuation in the community that he founded, the church, is the actual *agent* of reconciliation. This move is theologically significant for several reasons.

First, Schleiermacher, in the tradition of his Reformed forebears, puts the Word of God at the center of his whole system of theology. The incarnate Word (*das fleischgewordene Wort*) is the sine qua non of reconciliation. For Anselm and Calvin, the incarnation represents merely the necessary prerequisite for atonement. (Otherwise, why would Anselm have to ask the question, Why the God-man?) For Schleiermacher, the incarnation itself is the beginning of the regeneration of the whole human race. Christ, as the Word incarnate, communicates to humanity the blessedness that he shares with his Father, and disperses this blessing with his Spirit in the church. Schleiermacher does not reduce the Word of God to the words of scripture any more than Calvin did. The Word in the person of Jesus and in the preaching of the church is truly *God's* Word—not a human possibility or achievement, but "the supreme divine revelation."[13] For this reason, the neo-orthodox allegation that Schleiermacher substituted the word of man for the Word of God is entirely untenable.

Second, Schleiermacher's doctrine of the Word as the instrument of reconciliation makes a more coherent connection between Christology and soteriology. To believe is to be taken up by the Word of God and so united with Christ that we share the strength of his consciousness of God. Or, to put this in less technical language, faith is grounded in hearing the Word of God as disclosed in the preaching of Jesus and consequently sharing with Christ himself the relationship to and awareness of God that this preaching speaks of. Originally, individuals were grasped by the words of the human Jesus, but even now it is the work of Christ, mediated by his presence in the proclaimed Word, that takes hold of people and grants them participation in the new life.[14] Thus, the work of Christ is always the same; only the mode of his presence has changed. Like the first disciples, present-day believers are encountered by the being of Christ in the proclaimed Word, and the impression he makes on them reconciles them with God. Schleiermacher, then, unlike Calvin, does not have a problem relating a work of Christ in the past with the work of the *Christus praesens*, a work *extra nos* and a work *in nobis*. For Schleiermacher, these are one and the same.

Finally, Schleiermacher's understanding of the work of Christ makes it possible for him to decrease dramatically the number of historical claims on which faith relies. Since it is the Word of Christ, and not his virgin birth, death, resurrection, or ascension that brings about salvation, Schleiermacher can be largely indifferent to what historians may conclude about these events, or supposed events. Ultimately, faith demands only one past event, namely, *that* the incarnation happened, or, as he puts it in *Gl.* § 93, that the ideal became completely historical in Christ. Now this is no small claim, and it is undoubtedly just as problematic from a historian's point of view as are stories about resurrection from the dead.[15] But Schleiermacher does not need to verify even this claim historically: it is a postulate of Christian faith.[16] In the experience of Christians in the church, the actuality of the incarnation, properly understood, is a fact: a new principle has been introduced into the world that is gradually overcoming the darkness of sin. It is, of course, arguable that Schleiermacher's language about the sinless perfection of Christ implied by the new principle is inflated and unwarranted. But for present-day Christians, the historical anchor point of faith is precisely in the church of the present, where Christ is encountered daily in the Word, and not in some distant and scarcely retrievable historical event of the past.[17]

By placing the sacramental Word at the center of his Christology, soteriology, and ecclesiology, then, Schleiermacher achieved a significant improvement over Calvin's systematics. He makes the connections between the various loci more coherent, and he avoids the most troublesome questions that historical criticism might raise for a modern theologian. But in so revising his Christology, Schleiermacher was not abandoning his Reformation heritage. On the contrary, he was thoroughly applying the principles *sola gratia* and *sola fide*: faith comes by hearing "the preaching of Christ" (Rom. 10:17, RSV). Jesus Christ is the Word made flesh. His redemptive activity on our behalf can only be understood as the work of an efficacious Word.

## THE SACRAMENTAL WORD
## IN TWENTIETH-CENTURY THEOLOGY

The concept of the sacramental Word underwent something of a renaissance in twentieth-century theology. Several factors worked to produce this result. First, developments in form criticism of the New Testament made it seem ever more impossible to get behind the New Testament text to the Jesus of history. While for some this was a cause for alarm, for other theologians it presented an opportunity to reassess the significance of the "Gospel history" for Christian faith. Second, the dialectical theology, in its criticism of the easy identification of gospel and culture, became increasingly intrigued with the doctrine of the Word as an antidote. Third, the influence of existential philosophy on theology in the first half of the century led to a fresh appropriation of the concept of "event" in language about the Word. Theologians no longer spoke about the Word as a static text, but about dynamic "Word events" that encountered individuals and demanded their decision. Finally, developments in Roman Catholic theology after Vatican II, as well as increased ecumenical exchanges, led Catholic theologians to affirm a doctrine of the sacramental Word.[18] More needs to be done on both the concept of the sacramental Word and its implications for the vexed question of the historical Jesus. But its fruitfulness and further possibilities seem clear.

Karl Barth spoke profoundly about the problem of preaching in his early essays from the 1920s. In "The Need and Promise of Christian Preaching," he describes the situation when the minister ascends the pulpit on Sunday morning to preach. There is an expectation that God himself will speak to the congregation: "God is present! God *is* present. The whole situation witnesses, cries, simply shouts of it, even when in minister or people there arises questioning, wretchedness, or despair."[19] This understanding of preaching, Barth argues, is the *only* sacrament left to the evangelical churches after the Reformation. But Barth also highlights the difficulty of the concept:

> God's Word on human lips: that is not possible, it does not happen, that is not something one can set his sights on and make to take place. For it is *God's* action toward which the expectancy of heaven and earth is directed. Nothing else can satisfy the waiting people and nothing else can be the will of God than that he himself should be the one who acts. But the word of God is and will and must be and remain the word of *God*. When it appears to be something else—even something most brilliant and Christian and biblical—it has turned into its opposite.[20]

To avoid a confusion of the Word of God with the human word, it is necessary, Barth insists, to recognize God's sovereign freedom to speak when and where and with whom God will. Humans cannot control or conjure the Word of God. In his essay "The Word of God as the Task of Theology," Barth concludes: "We ought therefore to recognize both that we should speak of God and yet cannot, and by that very recognition give God the glory."[21] He warns his readers that "as a Reformed churchman . . . I have a duty to keep my sure distance from the Lutheran *est*."[22] The sign is not the thing signified.

Barth's reluctance to recognize an intrinsic connection between the sign and the thing signified may perhaps place him closer to Zwingli than to Calvin. For Calvin, as we have seen, insists that the proclaimed Word and sacraments are the regular and ordinary means by which God is committed to communicate grace to the elect. While Calvin too, in his rejection of Roman Catholic sacramental theology, argued that humans could not control God's grace, he nonetheless insisted that God had bound himself by his own promise to make grace regularly available in Word and sacrament. It may be scandalous to assert that God's Word is on the lips of "a puny man risen up from the dust," but in fact God's Word comes in this way all the time. Barth's rhetoric, on the contrary, seems to suggest that God's appearance in the Word is an unpredictable, extrinsic occurrence. As does Zwingli, Barth argues that God is absolutely free, not committed in any respect to use instruments for communicating grace.[23]

Barth does, however, recognize the way in which proclamation makes the events of the "Gospel history" contemporaneous with the hearer. In a fascinating autobiographical reminiscence in the *Church Dogmatics* he states:

> [Abel Burckhardt's children's songs] were the textbook from which I received my first theological instruction at the beginning of the last decade of the 19th century, in a form which was appropriate for my immature years. What made an indelible impression on me was the homely self-assurance with which these unpretentious verses spoke of the events of Christmas, Palm Sunday, Good Friday, Easter, Ascension, Pentecost, as though they could have taken place that very morning in Basel or nearby, like any other exciting event. History? Doctrine? Dogma? Myth? No. It was all things actually taking place. You could see everything for yourself, listen to it and take it to heart by hearing one of these songs, sung in the language you were hearing elsewhere and beginning to speak, and you could join the song yourself. Holding your mother's hand you went to the stable in Bethlehem, along the streets of Jerusalem, into which the savior was making his entry, hailed by children of your own age. You climbed the grim hill of Golgotha and walked in Joseph's garden at daybreak. . . . Was it all rather naive? . . . Indeed it was very naive, but perhaps the deepest wisdom, with its fullest force, lies in naivety, and this kind of wisdom, once gained, can carry a man over whole oceans of historicism and anti-historicism, mysticism and rationalism, orthodoxy, liberalism, and existentialism. He certainly will not be spared trial and temptation, but in the end he will be brought back relatively unscathed to firm ground.[24]

Even on this point, however, Barth is clear that the preacher cannot "make present" the narrated events, or exercise control over the Word of God: it remains a miracle of God's grace that the biblical texts become facts of our own experience.[25] Moreover, Barth is critical of the kerygmatic theology of Bultmann because it does not recognize that the kerygma points back to the *history* of Jesus Christ. It is the actual accomplishments of the Jesus of history that are spoken forth in the kerygma, and that authorize it.[26] In this sense John the Baptist is a reflection and prototype of all preachers: the Word points away from itself to the One who *has* come.[27]

Rudolf Bultmann approached the doctrine of the Word both as a New Testament scholar, deeply immersed in form criticism, and as a theologian intrigued by the application of categories from existential philosophy to the understanding of Christian faith. If Barth shied away from the Lutheran "est," Bultmann heartily embraced it. "Christ crucified and risen encounters us in the word of proclamation and nowhere else."[28] That is because

> the word of the Christian proclamation and the history it communicates coincide, are one. The history of Christ is not a history already past but one that takes place in the word being proclaimed. The remembrance of Jesus does not happen in such a way that he is remembered as Moses was, by remembering what he brought, what the people experienced through him and to which they are to be faithful. Rather, it is he himself who in the present word encounters the hearer, for whom the history itself now begins.[29]

*Christ* is so present in the *proclamation* that Bultmann can conceive of them as identical: the proclamation of the Word *is* the continuation of the Christ event—Christ is the proclamation.[30] And the event of Jesus' presence in the Word is encountered even without faith to receive it, to the judgment of those who reject him.[31]

Karl Rahner, in his essay "Word and Eucharist," argues that the current crisis in preaching awakens the need for a *theology* of preaching. This should not be a purely technical explanation of rhetoric and homiletic, but a theological explication of the proclaimed Word of God.[32] He thinks that the Protestants of the nineteenth century tended to see preaching as everything and the sacraments as purely traditional relics added to the preaching of pure doctrine (*reine Lehre*). But the Catholics, on their side, underestimated the importance of the Word and regarded it as nothing more than an unavoidable preparation for the sacraments.[33] To redress this imbalance, Rahner explicates a Catholic doctrine of the sacramentality of the Word. What guarantees the character of the Word as Word *of God* is the fact that it is proclaimed in the church.[34] The Word of God in the church is an inner impulse of God's saving activity toward humanity. It participates in the particularity of God's saving activity in Christ and the church.[35] Because the Word itself is powerful for salvation, we can assert that it brings what it declares and so is itself a saving event. The Word makes present the grace of God.[36] Rahner recognizes that this language may sound strange or unusual at first glance to his Catholic audience. But he insists that Roman Catholic theology has always recognized the exhibitive efficacy of the Word of God. When repentance and forgiveness are proclaimed in the church, they are not simply spoken about, but are actually experienced as events.[37]

Rahner qualifies his account, however, by insisting that not every word spoken in the church is equally sacramental.[38] And here he draws a distinction that makes his doctrine of the sacramental Word quite different from those of the Protestant theologians we have mentioned. In short, he insists that "the Eucharist is the absolute sacrament of the Word, the absolute case of the Word in general."[39] The Eucharist has this special place because it participates in the incarnation (through the *opus operatum* of the consecration) and because it is the eschatological proclamation of the original kerygma of the death of Christ.[40] In his emphasis on the Word of God *in the church*, and in his identification of the Sacrament of the altar as the highest form of the Word, Rahner faithfully represents his Roman Catholic tradition. But it is remarkable to note the degree of convergence he can find with evangelical theologians about the preached Word as a means of grace.

The idea of the sacramental Word has been an enormously fruitful one in the theology of the twentieth century. It has managed to bridge gaps between churches that are otherwise separated by the accretions of centuries of dogmatic differences. Moreover, the notion of the Word as sacrament has contributed to rethinking other doctrines, such as Christology, that have faced troubling challenges in the modern world. But what can it say to the preacher facing the gathered congregation from the pulpit?

## THE SACRAMENTAL WORD
## AND THE TASK OF PREACHING

Calvin claimed that his purpose in writing the *Institutes* was "to prepare and instruct candidates in sacred theology for the reading of the divine Word,"[41] and Schleiermacher insisted that "the dogmatic procedure has reference entirely to preaching, and only exists in the interests of preaching."[42] A doctrine is only as good as the help that it provides for the task of "rightly dividing the Word of truth" in the pulpit. If the challenges presented to Christian faith by historical criticism seemed grave in the middle of the nineteenth century, they appear even more ominous now. Not only is the history of Jesus the subject of intense scrutiny and ruthless criticism, but also the entire canon seems increasingly to be coming unraveled through biblical scholarship's constant tugging at the threads of its fabric. There have been many attempts in recent years to hold back the apparent destructiveness that the critical spirit unleashes on Christian faith. Narrative theology, canonical criticism, and even the focus on present experience in the various black, feminist, and liberation theologies may all be seen as creative responses to the erosive tendencies of historical criticism.

In this study, I have tried to recover an aspect of Reformed theology that seems particularly useful for preaching in these difficult times. The theology of the sacramental Word frees preachers from the historian's constraints and allows them to treat the putatively historical narratives of the Bible as themselves the disclosure of the present Christ. Preaching in the Reformed tradition is not primarily *didactic* but *sacramental:* it is a means of grace, not simply a method of instruction. We have seen Calvin and Schleiermacher blithely ignoring the history behind the text of scripture in their preaching. They did this neither out of ignorance nor out of fear, but rather in the firm conviction that the gospel itself, as witnessed in scripture and preaching, brings about the reconciliation of God and humanity. The Christ who redeems us is present in the church today through the proclaimed Word.

I do not mean to suggest that candidates for the ministry should henceforth give up learning ancient languages and reading in the wealth of historical scholarship on the Bible.[43] That would be untrue to the Reformed tradition, and especially to the two theologians on whom this study is based. Historical-critical biblical scholarship has a significance for church theologians and pastors that reaches beyond the task of preaching to dogmatic theology and ethics. But as preachers move from text to sermon, the doctrine of the sacramental Word obliges them to let go of their focus on the past. The actuality of the saving event of Jesus Christ cannot be retrieved by historical investigation: it is a fact of present experience in the fellowship of believers.

Preachers ought certainly to do their exegetical homework, but they need not dwell on the historian's questions that probe behind the text. Whether particular words attributed to Jesus, for example, are his *ipsissima verba* is entirely irrelevant. The Gospel of John is as worthy a disclosure of the sacramental Word as is the Gospel of Mark, or even the source "Q" insofar as we can recover it. For the purpose of the biblical texts in preaching is not to reconstruct the life of the historical Jesus but to mediate a saving encounter with Christ. D. F. Strauss, then, appears to be vindicated in his judgment that historical criticism makes little difference for the task of preaching. As Calvin comments on Romans 10:8 (" 'The word is near you, on your lips and in your heart' [that is, the word of faith that we proclaim]"):

> Believers, therefore, derive notable consolation from this passage with regard to the certainty of the Word. For they may rest in it with as great security as they would in what they saw to be actually present.[44]

# NOTES

1. Karl Barth, *Die Wort Gottes und die Theologie*, 164–65.

2. *Comm. John* 7:33 (*CO* 47:178).

3. See Robert A. Peterson, *Calvin's Doctrine of the Atonement* (Phillipsburg, N.J.: Presbyterian & Reformed Publishing Co., 1983), for a discussion of Calvin's bewildering array of metaphors for the atonement.

4. John F. Jansen, *Calvin's Doctrine of the Work of Christ* (London: J. Clarke, 1956), 90. Peterson argues that there are three main metaphors for atonement: Christ the Victor, Christ as Legal Substitute, and Christ as Sacrifice (*Calvin's Doctrine of the Atonement*, 55). All of them, in my judgment, share to some degree the same problem of coherence with Calvin's soteriology.

5. *Inst.*, 3.1.1. This is the passage I use as the first epigraph for this chapter.

6. See Paul van Buren, *Christ in Our Place: The Substitutionary Character of Calvin's Doctrine of Reconciliation* (Edinburgh: Oliver & Boyd, 1957), 32; B. A. Gerrish, "Atonement and 'Saving Faith,'" *Theology Today* 17 (July 1960): 184.

7. Of course, it is important to remember the role of the Holy Spirit as the bond of believers' union with Christ. For Calvin himself, the Holy Spirit may have played the role of linking Christology and soteriology, or objective and subjective atonement. Nonetheless, I do not believe this solves the logical inconsistency between the concept of reconciliation itself argued one way in book 2 and a rather different way in book 3.

8. *Inst.*, 2.15, on the threefold office of Christ.

9. *Gl.*, §§ 27, 95.

10. See pp. 60–65 above.

11. *Serm. John 15:1–7* (SW II/9:469–83, esp. 475–79); cf. *Das Leben Jesu* (SW I/6:348).

12. *CO* 46:870–71. The distinction between the offices of minister of the Word and Redeemer of the world do not seem to match up precisely with the distinction between the three offices of Christ—prophet, priest, and king—that Calvin discusses in *Inst.* 2.15. It seems he is speaking of a different matter here.

13. *Gl.*, § 14.Zusatz (ET, 72).

14. *Gl.*, § 106.2. This is the passage I chose for the second epigraph to this chapter.

15. D. F. Strauss argues this powerfully in his *Life of Jesus*, 768–73.

16. It was D. F. Strauss who, in criticism of Schleiermacher's Christology, maintained that as the existence of God was for Kant a postulate of the practical reason, so the dogma of Christ was for Schleiermacher a postulate of Christian experience (*Charakteristiken und Kritiken: Eine Sammlung zerstreuten Aufsätze aus den Gebieten der Theologie, Anthropologie und Aesthetik*, 2d impression (Leipzig: Otto Wigand, 1844), 41.

17. See Hayo Gerdes, "Anmerkungen zur Christologie der Glaubenslehre Schleiermachers," *Neue Zeitschrift für systematische Theologie und Religionsphilosophie* 25 (1983): 112–25, esp. 122ff.

18. See the articles on "Kerygma" in *Die Religion in Geschichte und Gegenwart*, 3:1250–54, and *Evangelisches Kirchenlexikon: Internationale theologische Enzyklopädie*, ed. Erwin Fahlbusch, Jan Milič Lochman, John Mbiti, Jaroslav Pelikan, Lukas Vischer, et al., 3d ed., 4 vols. (Göttingen: Vandenhoeck & Ruprecht, 1986–), 2: 1029–30.

19. *Die Wort Gottes und die Theologie*, 105.

20. *Die Wort Gottes und die Theologie*, 117–18.

21. *Die Wort Gottes und die Theologie*, 175.

22. *Die Wort Gottes und die Theologie*, 178. Although Barth wanted to avoid Luther's apparent identification of the sign and the thing signified, it is interesting that Barth's favorite phrase for describing God's freedom to work through signs only when it pleases him (*Ubi et quando visum est Deo*) is taken from the Augsburg Confession (*The Book of Concord: The Confessions of the Evangelical Lutheran Church*, trans. and ed. Theodore G. Tappert et al. [Philadelphia: Fortress Press, 1959], 31).

23. For Zwingli's view of divine freedom from the use of instruments, see his *Fidei ratio* (1530), in *Huldreich Zwinglis sämtliche Werke*, ed. Emil Egli et al., *Corpus Reformatorum*, vols. 88ff. (Berlin, 1905-), 6,2:803–4.

24. Karl Barth, *Die kirchliche Dogmatik* (Zurich: Evangelischer Verlag, 1955), 4/2:125. Hereafter cited as *KD*.

25. The affinity with Zwinglian ideas is again striking. B. A. Gerrish notes that Zwingli had a "'Barthian' dread of putting God at man's disposal" (*The Old Protestantism and the New*, 129).

26. *KD* 4/2:231.

27. *KD* 4/2:232. Again, Barth's insistence that the Word points to past history—the history of Jesus—perhaps sounds more like Zwinglian memorialism than Calvinist instrumentalism. For Zwingli, signs are not instrumental but declarative: they point to something God has done and they declare the intention of the recipient to live in accord with God's act (*Fidei ratio* [1530], *Huldreich Zwinglis sämtliche Werke*, 6,2:804–5).

28. H. W. Bartsch, *Kerygma und Mythos*, 2d ed. (Hamburg: Herbert Reich Evangelischer Verlag, 1951), 1:46.

29. Rudolf Bultmann, *Glauben und Verstehen*, 2d ed. (Tübingen: J.C.B. Mohr [Paul Siebeck], 1954), 1:292–93.

30. *Glauben und Verstehen*, 1:289–90.

31. *Glauben und Verstehen*, 2:258. This, too, is like Luther's teaching on the sacraments. While Calvin thought that the gift of the sacraments could not be received without faith, though it is given to all, Luther argued that even the wicked receive the body and blood of Christ to their damnation.

32. Karl Rahner, *Schriften zur Theologie*, vol. 4 (Zurich: Benziger Verlag, 1964), 315–16.

33. Rahner, *Schriften zur Theologie*, 4:317.

34. Ibid., 318.

35. Ibid., 320.

36. Ibid., 321.

37. Ibid., 323–25.

38. Ibid., 326ff.

39. Ibid., 351.

40. Ibid., 351–55.

41. "Ioannes Calvinus Lectori," *OS* 3:6.

42. *Gl.*, § 19.1 (ET, 88).

43. To obviate any possible misunderstanding, I should perhaps stress that the historical problem with which this study is concerned is the problem of the his-

torical Jesus. I would by no means wish to question the pertinence of historical and linguistic competence for the exegesis and exposition of New Testament texts. Schleiermacher was no more inclined than Calvin to slight the importance of humanistic learning for preachers of the gospel.

44. *Comm. Rom.* 10:8 (*CO* 49:200).

# BIBLIOGRAPHY

## SOURCES AND TRANSLATIONS

Augustine. *In Joannis Evangelium Tractatus. Patrologiae cursus completus, series Latina*. Edited by J. P. Migne. 221 vols. Paris, 1844–1900. Volume 35.

Calvin, John. *Calvin's New Testament Commentaries*. Edited by David W. Torrance and Thomas F. Torrance. 12 vols. Grand Rapids: Wm. B. Eerdmans Publishing Co., 1959–72.

———. *Calvin's Tracts and Treatises*. Translated by Henry Beveridge. 3 vols. Edinburgh, 1844–51. Reprint, Grand Rapids: Wm. B. Eerdmans Publishing Co., 1958.

———. *The Commentaries of John Calvin*. 46 vols. Edinburgh: Calvin Translation Society, 1843–55. Reprint, 22 vols. Grand Rapids: Baker Book House, 1979.

———. *The Deity of Christ and Other Sermons*. Translated by Leroy Nixon. Grand Rapids: Wm. B. Eerdmans Publishing Co., 1950.

———. *Institutes of the Christian Religion*. Translated by Ford Lewis Battles. Edited by John T. McNeill. Library of Christian Classics, vols. 20–21. Philadelphia: Westminster Press, 1960.

———. *Ioannis Calvini opera quae supersunt omnia*. Edited by Wilhelm Baum, Eduard Cunitz, and Eduard Reuss. 59 vols. *Corpus Reformatorum*, vols. 29–87. Brunswick: C. A. Schwetschke & Son (M. Bruhn), 1863–1900.

———. *Ioannis Calvini Opera Selecta*. Edited by Peter Barth, Wilhelm Niesel, and Doris Scheuner. 5 vols. Munich: Chr. Kaiser Verlag, 1926–52.

*Canons and Decrees of the Council of Trent: Original Text with English Translation*. Translated by H. J. Schroeder, O.P. St. Louis: B. Herder Books, 1941.

*The Creeds of Christendom*. Edited by Philip Schaff. 3 vols. New York: Harper, 1877; 4th ed., 1919.

Luther, Martin. *D. Martin Luthers Werke: Kritische Gesamtausgabe*. Weimar: H. Böhlaus Nachfolger, 1883–.

———. *Luther's Works*. Edited by Jaroslav Pelikan and Helmut T. Lehmann. 55 vols. St. Louis: Concordia Publishing House; Philadelphia: Fortress Press, 1955–76.

*Melanchthon and Bucer*. Translated and edited by Wilhelm Pauck. Library of Christian Classics, vol. 19. Philadelphia: Westminster Press, 1969.

Schleiermacher, Friedrich Daniel Ernst. *Aus Schleiermachers Leben in Briefen*. Edited by Ludwig Jonas and Wilhelm Dilthey. 4 vols. Berlin: Georg Reimer, 1858–63.

———. *Brief Outline on the Study of Theology*. Translated by Terrence N. Tice. Richmond: John Knox Press, 1966.

————. *The Christian Faith.* Translated from the 2d German edition. Edited by H. R. Mackintosh and J. S. Stewart. Philadelphia: Fortress Press, 1976.

————. *Der christliche Glaube nach den Grundsätzen der evangelischen Kirche im Zusammenhange dargestellt.* 7th edition, based on the 2d edition. Edited by Martin Redeker. 2 vols. Berlin: Walter de Gruyter, 1960.

————. *A Critical Essay on the Gospel of Luke.* Translated by Connop Thirlwall. London: John Taylor, 1825.

————. *Friedrich Schleiermachers Reden über die Religion.* Edited by G. Ch. Bernhard Pünjer. Brunswick: C. A. Schwetschke & Son (M. Bruhn), 1879.

————. *Friedrich Schleiermachers sämmtliche Werke.* 31 vols. Berlin: Georg Reimer, 1834–64.

————. *Hermeneutics: The Handwritten Manuscripts.* Translated by James Duke and Jack Forstman. Edited by Heinz Kimmerle. American Academy of Religion Texts and Translations Series, no. 1. Missoula, Mont.: Scholars Press, 1977.

————. *Hermeneutik, nach den Handschriften neu herausgegeben und eingeleitet.* Edited by Heinz Kimmerle. Heidelberger Akademie der Wissenschaffen, Philosophisch-Historische Klasse, Abhandlung 2. Heidelberg: Carl Winter, 1959.

————. *Kritische Gesamtausgabe.* Edited by Hans-Joachim Birkner, Gerhard Ebeling, Hermann Fischer, Heinz Kimmerle, Kurt-Victor Selge. Berlin: Walter de Gruyter, 1984–.

————. *Kurze Darstellung des theologischen Studiums zum Behuf einleitender Vorlesungen.* 3d ed. Edited by Heinrich Scholz. Leipzig: A. Deichert, 1910.

————. *The Life of Jesus.* Translated by S. Maclean Gilmour. Edited by Jack C. Verheyden. Philadelphia: Fortress Press, 1975.

————. *On the Glaubenslehre: Two Letters to Dr. Lücke.* Translated by James Duke and Francis S. Fiorenza. American Academy of Religion Texts and Translations Series, no. 3. Chico, Calif.: Scholars Press, 1981.

————. *On Religion: Speeches to Its Cultured Despisers.* Translated from the 1st German edition by Richard Crouter. Cambridge: Cambridge University Press, 1988.

————. *On Religion: Speeches to Its Cultured Despisers.* Translated from the 3d German edition by John Oman. New York: Harper & Row, 1958.

————. *Schleiermachers Sendschreiben über seine Glaubenslehre an Lücke.* Edited by Hermann Mulert. Giessen: Töpelmann, 1908.

————. *Servant of the Word: Selected Sermons of Friedrich Schleiermacher.* Translated and edited by Dawn DeVries. Philadelphia: Fortress Press, 1987.

————. *Werke: Auswahl in vier Bänden.* Edited by Otto Braun and Johannes Bauer. Leipzig, 1927–28. Reprint, Hamburg: Felix Meiner, 1967.

Zwingli, Huldreich. *Huldreich Zwinglis sämtliche Werke.* Edited by Emil Egli et al. *Corpus Reformatorum,* vols. 88ff. Berlin, 1905–.


## SECONDARY LITERATURE

Arens, Edmund, ed. *Habermas und die Theologie.* Düsseldorf: Patmos, 1989.

Arndt, Andreas, and Wolfgang Virmond, eds. *Schleiermachers Briefwechsel (Verzeichnis) nebst einer Liste seiner Vorlesungen.* Schleiermacher Archiv, vol. 11. Berlin: Walter de Gruyter, 1992.

Backus, Irena, and Francis Higman, eds. *Théorie et pratique de l'exégèse: Actes du*

*troisième colloque international sur l'histoire de l'exégèse biblique au XVIe siècle.*
Geneva: Droz, 1990.

Barth, Karl. *Homiletics.* Translated by Geoffrey W. Bromiley and Donald E.
Daniels. Louisville, Ky.: Westminster/John Knox Press, 1991.

————. *Die kirchliche Dogmatik.* Vol. 4/2. Zurich: Evangelischer Verlag, 1955.

————. *Protestant Theology in the Nineteenth Century: Its Background and History.*
Valley Forge, Pa.: Judson Press, 1973.

————. *Die Theologie Schleiermachers: Vorlesungen Göttingen, Wintersemester 1923/
24.* Edited by Dietrich Ritschl. Zurich: Theologischer Verlag, 1978.

————. *Die Theologie und die Kirche.* Munich: Chr. Kaiser Verlag, 1928.

————. *Theology and the Church.* Translated by Louise Pettibone Smith. London:
SCM Press, 1962.

————. *The Theology of Schleiermacher: Lectures at Göttingen, Winter Semester of
1923/24.* Translated by Geoffrey W. Bromiley. Edited by Dietrich Ritschl. Grand
Rapids: Wm. B. Eerdmans Publishing Co., 1982.

————. *The Word of God and the Word of Man.* Translated by Douglas Horton. London: Hodder & Stoughton, 1928.

————. *Das Wort Gottes und die Theologie.* Munich: Chr. Kaiser Verlag, 1924.

Bartsch, H. W. *Kerygma und Mythos.* 2d ed. Hamburg: Herbert Reich evangelischer
Verlag, 1951.

Bauer, Johannes. *Schleiermacher als patriotischer Prediger.* Giessen: Töpelmann, 1908.

————, ed. *Ungedruckte Predigten Schleiermachers aus den Jahren 1820–1828.* Leipzig:
M. Heinsius Nachfolger, 1909.

Bavaud, Georges. "Les Rapports entre la prédication et les sacrements dans le contexte du dialogue oecumenique." In *Communion et communication: Structures
d'unité et modèles de communication de l'évangile. Troisième Cycle romand en théologie practique (1976–77).* Geneva: Labor et Fides, 1978.

Bizer, Ernst. *Fides ex auditu: Eine Untersuchung über die Entdeckung der Gerechtigkeit
Gottes durch Martin Luther.* Neukirchen: Verlag der Buchhandlung des Erziehungsvereins, 1958.

Bleek, Hermann. *Die Grundlage der Christologie Schleiermachers: Eine Entwicklung der
Anschauungsweise Schleiermachers bis zur Glaubenslehre, mit besonderer Rücksicht
auf seine Christologie.* Tübingen: J.C.B. Mohr, 1898.

Bouwsma, William J. *John Calvin: A Sixteenth Century Portrait.* New York: Oxford
University Press, 1988.

Brunner, Heinrich Emil. *Die Mystik und das Wort: Der Gegensatz zwischen moderner
Religionsauffassung und christlichem Glauben dargestellt an der Theologie Schleiermachers.* Tübingen: J.C.B. Mohr, 1924.

Bultmann, Rudolf. *Glauben und Verstehen.* 2d ed. Tübingen: J.C.B. Mohr (Paul
Siebeck), 1954.

Buren, Paul van. *Christ in Our Place: The Substitutionary Character of Calvin's Doctrine of Reconciliation.* Edinburgh: Oliver & Boyd, 1957.

Daniélou, Jean. *Origen.* Translated by W. Mitchell. New York: Sheed & Ward, 1955.

Davison, James E. "Can God Speak a Word to Man? Barth's Critique of Schleiermachers Theology," *Scottish Journal of Theology* 37 (1984): 189–211.

Delumeau, Jean. *Catholicism between Luther and Voltaire: A New View of the Counter-
Reformation.* Translated by Jeremy Moiser. London: Burns & Oates, 1977.

DeVries, Dawn. "Schleiermacher's Christmas Eve Dialogue: Bourgeois Ideology
or Feminist Theology?" *Journal of Religion* 69 (1989): 169–83.

Dominicé, Max. "Die Christusverkündigung bei Calvin." In *Jesus Christus im Zeugnis der heiligen Schrift und der Kirche*. Eine Vortragsreihe von Dr. R. L. Schmidt, Dr. E. Gaugler, Dr. R. Bultmann, Dr. U. Gelg, Dr. E. Wolf, and M. Dominicé. 2d ed. Munich: Chr. Kaiser Verlag, 1936.

Douglass, E. Jane Dempsey. *Justification in Late Medieval Preaching: A Study of John Geiler of Keisersberg*. 2d ed. Leiden: E. J. Brill, 1989.

Duke, James O., and Robert F. Streetman, eds. *Barth and Schleiermacher: Beyond the Impasse?* Philadelphia: Fortress Press, 1988.

*Evangelisches Kirchenlexikon: Internationale theologische Enzyklopädie*. Edited by Erwin Fahlbusch, Jan Milič Lochmann, John Mbiti, Jaroslav Pelikan, Lukas Vischer, et al. 3d ed. 4 vols. Göttingen: Vandenhoeck & Ruprecht, 1986–.

Forstman, H. Jackson. *Word and Spirit: Calvin's Doctrine of Biblical Authority*. Stanford, Calif.: Stanford University Press, 1962.

Frei, Hans W. *The Eclipse of the Biblical Narrative: A Study in Eighteenth and Nineteenth Century Hermeneutics*. New Haven, Conn.: Yale University Press, 1974.

Ganoczy, Alexandre. *Ecclesia Ministrans: Dienende Kirche und kirchlicher Dienst bei Calvin*. Freiburg: Herder, 1968.

————— and Stefan Scheld. *Die Hermeneutik Calvins: Geistesgeschichtliche Voraussetzungen und Grundzüge*. Veröffentlichungen des Instituts für Europäische Geschichte Mainz, vol. 114. Wiesbaden: Franz Steiner Verlag, 1983.

George, Timothy, ed. *John Calvin and the Church: A Prism of Reform*. Louisville, Ky.: Westminster/John Knox Press, 1990.

Gerdes, Hayo. "Anmerkungen zur Christologie der Glaubenslehre Schleiermachers." *Neue Zeitschrift für systematische Theologie und Religionsphilosophie* 25 (1983): 112–25.

Gerrish, B. A. "Atonement and 'Saving Faith.'" *Theology Today* 17 (1960): 181–91.

—————. *Continuing the Reformation: Essays on Modern Religious Thought*. Chicago: University of Chicago Press, 1993.

—————. *Grace and Gratitude: The Eucharistic Theology of John Calvin*. Minneapolis: Fortress Press, 1992.

—————. *The Old Protestantism and the New: Essays on the Reformation Heritage*. Chicago: University of Chicago Press, 1982.

—————. *A Prince of the Church: Schleiermacher and the Beginnings of Modern Theology*. Philadelphia: Fortress Press, 1984.

—————. "The Reformers' Theology of Worship." *McCormick Quarterly* 14 (1961): 21–29.

—————. *Tradition and the Modern World: Reformed Theology in the Nineteenth Century*. Chicago: University of Chicago Press, 1978.

Grützmacher, Richard H. *Wort und Geist: Eine historische und dogmatische Untersuchung zum Gnadenmittel des Wortes*. Leipzig: A. Deichert'sche Verlagsbuchhandlung (Georg Böhme), 1902.

Harnack, Adolf von. *History of Dogma*. Translated from the 3d German edition by Neil Buchanan. 7 vols. London, 1900. Reprint, Gloucester, Mass.: Peter Smith, 1976.

Hirsch, Emanuel. *Schleiermachers Christusglaube: Drei Studien*. Gütersloh: Mohn, 1968.

Hunt, R. N. Carew. *Calvin*. London: Centenary Press, 1933.

Jansen, John F. *Calvin's Doctrine of the Work of Christ*. London: James Clarke, 1956.

Jung, K. G. *Der Erlösungsbegriff der frühen Predigten F.D.E. Schleiermachers*. Ph.D. thesis, University of Berlin, 1971.

Kiessling, Elmer Carl. *The Early Sermons of Luther and Their Relation to the Pre-Reformation Sermon.* Grand Rapids: Zondervan, 1935.

Köhlbing, P. "Schleiermachers Zeugnis vom Sohne Gottes nach seinen Festpredigten." *Zeitschrift für Theologie und Kirche* 3 (1893): 277–310.

Kolfhaus, Wilhelm. *Christusgemeinschaft bei Johannes Calvin.* Neukirchen: Buchhandlung des Erziehungsvereins, 1938.

Krotz, F. *Predigt und Glaube: F. Schleiermacher über Christi Liebe.* Ph.D. thesis, Marburg University, 1974.

Lange, D. *Historische Jesus oder mythischer Christus: Untersuchungen zu dem Gegensatz Zwischen F. Schleiermacher und D. F. Strauss.* Gütersloh: Mohn, 1975.

Lewis, Alan E. "Ecclesia ex auditu: A Reformed View of the Church as the Community of the Word of God." *Scottish Journal of Theology* 35 (1982): 13–31.

Lütz, Dietmar. *Homo Viator: Karl Barths Ringen mit Schleiermacher.* Zurich: Theologischer Verlag, 1988.

Maxwell, William D. *An Outline of Christian Worship: Its Development and Forms.* London: Oxford University Press, 1936.

McNeill, John T. "The Significance of the Word of God for Calvin." *Church History* 28 (1959): 131–46.

Meding, Wichmann von, ed. *Bibliographie der Schriften Schleiermachers nebst einer Zusammenstellung und Datierung seiner gedruckten Predigten.* Schleiermacher Archiv, vol. 9. Berlin: Walter de Gruyter, 1992.

Meier-Dörken, Christoph. *Die Theologie der frühen Predigten Schleiermachers.* Berlin: Walter de Gruyter, 1988.

Melzer, Friso. "Christus in der Predigt Schleiermachers." *Theologische Studien und Kritiken* 104 (1932): 54–84.

Millet, Olivier. "Sermon sur la Résurrection: Quelques remarques sur l'homilétique de Calvin." *Bulletin de la Société de l'Histoire du Protestantisme Français* 134 (1988): 683–92.

Moretto, Giovanni. "Angezogen und belehrt von Gott: Der Johannismus in Schleiermachers 'Reden über die Religion.'" *Theologische Zeitschrift* 37 (1981): 267–91.

Mülhaupt, Erwin. *Die Predigt Calvins: Ihre Geschichte, ihre Form, und ihre Religiösen Grundgedanken.* Arbeiten zur Kirchengeschichte, vol. 18. Berlin and Leipzig: Walter de Gruyter, 1931.

Müller, Denis. "L'Element historique dans la prédication de Calvin: Un aspect original de l'homilétique du Réformateur." *Revue d'histoire et de philosophie religieuses* 64 (1984): 365–86.

Neuser, Wilhelm H., ed. *Calvinus Ecclesiae Genevensis Custos: International Congress on Calvin Research, 6–9 September 1982 in Geneva.* Frankfurt: Peter Lang, 1984.

———. *Calvinus Servus Christi: International Congress on Calvin Research, 25–28 August 1986 in Debrecen.* Budapest: Presseabteilung des Ráday-Kollegiums, 1988.

*New Catholic Encyclopedia.* Vol. 9. New York: McGraw-Hill Book Co., 1967.

*The New Schaff-Herzog Encyclopedia of Religious Knowledge.* Edited by Samuel Macauley Jackson et al. New York and London: Funk & Wagnalls, 1908–14.

Niebuhr, Richard R. *Schleiermacher on Christ and Religion.* London: SCM Press, 1964.

Nixon, Leroy. *John Calvin, Expository Preacher.* Grand Rapids: Wm. B. Eerdmans Publishing Co., 1950.

Ohst, Martin. *Schleiermacher und die Bekenntnisschriften: Eine Untersuchung zu seiner Reformations- und Protestantismusdeutung.* Tübingen: J.C.B. Mohr (Paul Siebeck), 1989.

Parker, T.H.L. *Calvin's New Testament Commentaries.* Grand Rapids: Wm. B. Eerdmans Publishing Co., 1971.

————. *Calvin's Preaching.* Louisville, Ky.: Westminster/John Knox Press, 1992.

————. *The Oracles of God: An Introduction to the Preaching of John Calvin.* London and Redhill: Lutterworth Press, 1947.

Peterson, Robert A. *Calvin's Doctrine of the Atonement.* Philipsburg, N.J.: Presbyterian & Reformed Publishing Co., 1983.

Quapp, E.H.U. *Barth contra Schleiermacher: "Die Weihnachtsfeier" als Nagelprobe.* Marburg: Karl Wenzel, 1978.

————. *Christus im Leben Schleiermachers: Vom Herrnhuter zum Spinozisten.* Göttingen: Vandenhoeck & Ruprecht, 1972.

Rahner, Karl. *Schriften zur Theologie.* Vol. 4. Zurich: Benziger Verlag, 1964.

Rainbow, Jonathon H. *The Will of God and the Cross: An Historical and Theological Study of John Calvin's Doctrine of Limited Redemption.* Allison Park, Pa.: Pickwick Publications, 1990.

Ravensway, J. Marius J. Lange van. *Augustinus totus noster: Das Augustinverständnis bei Johannes Calvin.* Göttingen: Vandenhoeck & Ruprecht, 1990.

*Die Religion in Geschichte und Gegenwart.* 3d ed. Edited by Hans Frhr. von Campenhausen et al. 6 vols. Tübingen: J.C.B. Mohr (Paul Siebeck), 1957–62.

Schellong, Dieter. *Calvins Auslegung der synoptischen Evangelien.* Munich: Chr. Kaiser Verlag, 1969.

Seeberg, Reinhold. *Textbook of the History of Doctrines.* Translated by Charles E. Hay. 2 vols. Grand Rapids: Baker Book House, 1952.

Selge, Kurt-Victor, ed. *Internationaler Schleiermacher-Kongress Berlin 1984.* Schleiermacher Archiv, vol. I.i–ii. Berlin: Walter de Gruyter, 1985.

Stauffer, Richard. *Dieu, la création et la Providence dans la prédication de Calvin.* Basler und Berner Studien zur historischen und systematischen Theologie, vol. 33. Bern: Peter Lang, 1978.

Strauss, David Friedrich. *Characteristiken und Kritiken: Eine Sammlung zerstreuten Aufsätzen aus den Gebieten der Theologie, Anthropologie und Aesthetik.* 2d impression. Leipzig: Otto Wigand, 1844.

————. *The Christ of Faith and the Jesus of History: A Critique of Schleiermacher's Life of Jesus.* Translated and edited by Leander E. Keck. Philadelphia: Fortress Press, 1977.

————. *Der Christus des Glaubens und der Jesus der Geschichte: Eine Kritik des Schleiermacher'schen Lebens Jesu.* Berlin, 1865. Reprint. Edited by Hans-Jürgen Geischer. Texte zur Kirchen- und Theologiegeschichte, vol. 14. Gütersloh: Gerd Mohn Verlagshaus, 1971.

————. *Das Leben Jesu, kritisch bearbeitet.* 2 vols. Tübingen: Verlag C. F. Osiander, 1835–36.

————. *The Life of Jesus Critically Examined.* Translated by George Eliot. 4th ed. Edited by Peter C. Hodgson. Philadelphia: Fortress Press, 1972.

Trillhaas, Wolfgang. *Schleiermachers Predigt und das homiletische Problem.* Berlin: Walter de Gruyter, 1931.

Wallace, Ronald S. *Calvin's Doctrine of the Word and Sacrament.* Edinburgh: Oliver & Boyd, 1953.

Wendland, Johannes. *Die religiöse Entwicklung Schleiermachers*. Tübingen: J.C.B. Mohr, 1915.

Willis, Edward D. *Calvin's Catholic Christology: The Function of the So-called extra-Calvinisticum in Calvin's Theology*. Leiden: E. J. Brill, 1966.

Zimmer, Friedrich. "Predigtentwürfe aus Friedrich Schleiermachers erster Amtsthätigkeit." *Zeitschrift für Praktische Theologie* 4 (1882): 281–90, 369–78.

Zink, Michel. *La Prédication en Langue Romane avant 1300*. Paris: Editions Honoré Champion, 1976.

# INDEX